D1600510

Trooper

by

David W. Moran

with

Richard F. Radford

Quinlan Press
Boston

Copyright © 1986
by Quinlan Press
All rights reserved,
including the right of reproduction
in whole or in part in any form.
Published by Quinlan Press
131 Beverly Street
Boston, MA 02114

Printed in the United States of America
August, 1986

Moran, David.
    Trooper.

    1. Moran, David. 2. Police, State—Massachusetts—
Biography. I. Radford, Dick. II. Title.
HV7911.M65A3   1986   363.2'092'4 [B]   85-60453
ISBN 0-933341-07-5

To Bill and Rita, who were responsible for my existence and set me on the right track. And to all those troopers, first in forest green and now in French and electric blue, who have ridden out on patrol.

D.M.

To my parents, Dick and Lorraine Radford, and the holy spirit that kept them in love ... and to Lynne, my wife of twenty years, in whom abides the same spirit.

D.R.

We would like to thank the following members of the Massachusetts State Police for their help and cooperation: Commissioner Frank J. Trabucco, Colonel Anthony J. Grillo, Lieutenant Colonel Robert E. Dunn, S/Sergeant John R. Bendonis, S/Sergeant Carmen Tammaro and Troopers Arthur MacDonald, Daniel J. Twomey, Andrew C. Palombo, David Webber and John J. Kelley. We are also indebted to the following people for their assistance: Lieutenant Richard Trahon and Reverend Mark Medina (chaplain) of the Brookline Police Department; John Crowley of the DEA; A.D.A. Joseph Killion; Captains Edward Finnerty and Paul Connaughton for their liaison work with Bill Wilson and Dr. Bob; Professor John J. Tobin of UMass; Kevin Stevens of Quinlan Press for editorial help; Louise Thompson and Jean Dwyer for electronic assistance; and Amy and Richard Radford for their valuable criticism and unfailing patience and humor. We also owe thanks to Boston Globe Newspapers, Inc., The Berkshire Eagle and the State Police Photography Bureau.

The events described in this book actually took place. Some names, dates and locations have been changed to protect the privacy of real persons.

1. The Academy

Getting in was the tough part...we thought.

Time: Spring, early 1960s
Location: State Police Academy, Framingham, Massachusetts
Duty: Survival

At precisely 0900 hours the front door of the old wooden administration building banged open. A lean, square-jawed drill instructor in knife-creased pants and spit and polish shoes strode toward us, clipboard jammed under his arm, campaign hat cocked menacingly over his flashing eyes. He stopped a measured five paces from the group, withering us with his stare. I stood with forty-nine other recruits, the gruelling Labor Day sun beating down on my newly shaven skull, Corporal Dzikiewicz's stern face reminding us of our lowly station. We sweated in our heavy civilian suits, waiting for orders.

The corporal designated us the Forty-fifth Recruit Training Troop, then barked his first command: "You hear your name called, you sound off." He began with the first name on our roster: "Ardini—Edward R."

"Here," Ardini answered, apprehensively.

"Here, what?" Corporal Dzikiewicz bellowed, his face inches from Ardini's timid mug.

Ardini was no dummy. He'd seen all the classic boot camp movies. He quickly rallied: "Here, *sir!*"

The corporal pointed to the oval track. "Take a lap, Ardini—on the double."

Ardini began running his first of a thousand quarter-mile laps at the academy, wondering what he'd said wrong. The corporal halted him, motioning to the recruit's luggage.

"Take your gear with you, Ardini. Next—Baron, Ronald," Corporal Dzikiewicz shouted, beginning on another recruit.

"Here, sir!" Baron answered, watching Ardini begin his luggage-laden run.

"Baron—the first word out of your mouth should always be 'sir'—you understand?"

Baron answered too quickly: "Yes sir!"

"Around the track!" Dzikiewicz sent a confused recruit Baron on his way, too. "Dunn, Robert E."

"Sir! Here, sir," Dunn responded correctly.

"That's better," the corporal beamed. The rest of us drew a relieved breath. "Ever in the military, Dunn?"

"Sir! Yes, sir."

The corporal seemed pleased. Thank God. This was like playing Simon says without knowing the rules. And none of us wanted to anger someone as exalted in the State Police hierarchy as this hard-to-please corporal.

"United States Marine Corps, sir," Dunn added, extemporaneously. Pushing his luck, we learned.

"Around the track, Dunn. I can't stand Marines."

And so it went. Nothing could satisfy Corporal Dzikiewicz. Each recruit ran, no matter what answer he gave. The track was soon littered with suitcases, seabags—luggage of every description. Our sixteen-week indoctrination had begun.

I consoled myself during those first laps with the thought of my success throughout the ruthless selection process. The fifty recruits on the parade field today had been winnowed down from five thousand original applicants. We had come through a comprehensive background check, a medical exam, a difficult written entrance exam taken on the famous parquet floor of the Boston Garden and a final, lengthy interview with seasoned veterans of the force.

I was beginning to weaken after a few laps, but the corporal was just getting his wind up. Looking like Boris Karloff, he kept up a nonstop bellow.

"You people make me sick. Can't do anything right—can't even run without dying. See that road?" He pointed his swagger stick toward a highway, visible through the chain link fence. "That's Route 9. It runs east and west, the entire length of the Commonwealth. Any of you civilians don't think you belong here, or can't cut the training, you're free to leave any time. Route 9 will get you close to home if you want to hit it. Personally, I don't think *any* of you belong here. Now, pick up your gear and move out. Let's see if you can march."

Another disaster. There were some others who, like me, hadn't had any army training and found the left-right business a bit confounding, but I became the goat.

"Halt!"

Corporal Dzikiewicz also tried *hold it, whoa* and *stop* before I got the message. That I proudly remembered to say "sir" first, when he asked my name, didn't appease Dzikiewicz.

"What'd you do in civilian life, Moran? Obviously you weren't in the military." I thought he was going to make me eat his swagger stick.

"Sir, no sir. I went to school, sir."

He threw up his hands. "Oh Christ, not another college boy?"

Dzikiewicz's contempt for higher education showed in his sneer. For the rest of our training cycle the corporal and several others on the staff would take great delight in reminding the college men in the class how little our education had prepared us for this experience. As if we needed reminding.

"Around the track, Moran—starting with your left foot."

It soon became apparent that no one, regardless of proficiency or physical condition, would escape the instructor's wrath. The saving thought was that nothing lasts forever.

The corporal marched us to a quonset hut. We learned that Massachusetts has the oldest state police in the United States, dating back to 1865. We learned that the training style and course format had changed little from a hundred years ago, when troopers rode horses and billeted in canvas tents. We learned that if we couldn't cut the training, there were plenty of alternates waiting to take our place.

In the hut we surveyed fifteen double bunks arranged in four rows. The two center rows were separated by a row of back-to-back wall lockers. Inside each locker a schematic drawing precisely detailed how we should arrange our uniform and other clothing.

We were assigned bunks and told to follow the schematic arrangement exactly. We had no sooner started when a voice on the P.A. system blared that we had two minutes to fall out in the company street in P.T. gear.

Needless to say, we moved much too slowly for the instructor. We had to practice falling out from the billets about thirty times until we got it right. After that we did a few miles around the track with the instructors leading. They hardly broke a sweat, but they sure knew how to bust aggies.

The noon trip to the mess hall was a waste of time—we were all too sick to eat, although we did consume gallons of water and "bug juice."

After lunch we went by bus to a local outdoor pool to qualify in swimming. Each candidate had to swim only fifty yards, a distance even the poorest swimmers could manage with enough determination and the encouragement of classmates, and I remember thinking that the staties must do all their business inland. It would be some time before my service on our scuba team disproved that prophecy.

The brief bus trip was our only rest break of that day. On our return we were hustled off the bus to perform calisthenics until we were nearly exhausted. It was at this point that several of the men then fell out, packed their gear and "hit Route 9," resigning from the State Police. But their departure that first day made me even more determined to hang in there, though I couldn't guarantee for how long.

The rest of the first day and evening we spent learning to make hospital corners on a bunk, getting an even shorter haircut and finding out how to make shoes shine like mirrors. At evening mess I still ate little. I remember looking around the room, wondering who would be the next to leave. I saw young men like myself from all corners of the Commonwealth, also eating tentatively, also wondering if they would make it.

I knew that it was academy policy to replace within hours any dropouts or failures during the first two weeks of a cycle. There was a waiting list of eager alternates, guys that had just missed getting into this class, who would be only too happy to fill a vacant slot, even if it meant playing catch-up. I didn't want my spot filled by anyone but me.

My private thoughts were ended by the instructor's whistle. Somehow most of us managed to drag ourselves up from the mess hall tables. We had a brisk run back to the barracks for more housekeeping lessons.

Retreat sounded at 2130 and then taps at exactly 2200 hours. Mentally and physically drained, I didn't have to be told twice to go to bed. I fell asleep immediately. My first day as a recruit was finally over.

Reveille broke the late summer silence at 0550 hours. With forty-five other tired recruits, I stirred in my bunk, unsure of where I was for a moment. I sat up and watched my upper berth neighbor, Arthur Scott, putting the finishing touches on his blanket. Neat and precise, Arthur pulled the edge of each side of the blanket under the mattress until it lined up on the third row of each wire bedspring. An inspecting officer looking up from below would see Scotty's symetrically placed blanket ends forming a perfect border.

Impressed by the precision, I thought, "I have a long way to go."

"Where did you learn that?" I asked.

Scott looked down and smiled easily. "I spent three years in the First Cavalry in Germany," he answered. "I can do this in my sleep. And hey...you'd better get your P.T. gear on. We fall out in two minutes."

I was lacing my sneakers when the P.A. system blared: "Outside! Outside!"

Three drill instructors dressed in P.T. gear watched the forty-six survivors from Day One trying to fit through the small door openings. Three of our classmates had left before retreat the previous evening. They didn't believe that they had what it takes to finish the sixteen weeks of recruit training.

Unhappy with the speed of the Forty-fifth Recruit Training Troop, the instructors played "in the building, out of the building" until our bodies glistened with sweat. After twenty grueling minutes the instructors seemed grudgingly satisfied with the performance of their new charges.

Now a program of calisthenics began, each instructor demonstrating an exercise and the military precision with which it should be performed.

"Gentlemen," he'd bellow, "the next exercise is the push-up. The push-up is a two-part exercise. You count the cadence, I count the repetitions. The beginning position is on your hands, elbows locked, knees flexed. OK, everyone on the deck."

After twenty minutes of push-ups, sit-ups, jumping jacks, squat thrusts and side-straddle-hops, we ran around the quarter-mile track twelve times, shouting cadence. One instructor set the pace. The other two followed the group, exhorting the stragglers to catch up with the main body. The dropouts were collected by the last instructor, who noted their names and advised them to report to him at 1230 hours. They became known as the Farouks, named after Egypt's fat king who reigned during the fifties. To be a Farouk meant skipping the noon meal and doing extra running, and P.T. Farouks soon looked as slim and fit as everyone else.

We spent the first two weeks living in sweat gear, doing P.T., marching and learning the calvary-inspired trooper jargon. "Saddle up," "mount" and "dismount" began to have meaning. Military drill and formations became less confusing as everyone began to settle in and learn the system. We wore khaki uniforms with a web belt and white WW II leggings laced over high black shoes. A Korean War "Ridgeway" cap provided "cover." The uniforms were starched and pressed.

As recruits dropped out of the class during this initial two-week period, new people took their places. They had to catch up and learn the system as best they could; sometimes they too dropped out after a few days. The rest of us knew that if we could make it through morning P.T., inspection and drill, we could survive another day, because most of the remaining time was now filled with classes or instruction. The atmosphere had relaxed a little.

During the fourth week of training, our morning routine began to vary. Every few days we got to tackle the obstacle or "confidence" course. Set away from the low quonset huts, it looked like a playground for giants. It had been put together with surplus telephone poles, placed in such a way that recruits had to climb up, jump over or hang from them in the most unnatural positions.

Most people felt queasiest on the cargo net. Designed to show people how to disembark from a ship into an amphibious craft, it consisted of two twenty-five foot telephone poles supporting a third pole stretched horizontally across the top. Over this pole hung a large cargo net. The object was to climb the net, swing over the top and climb down.

Then it happened. One of my classmates froze. The instructor ordered, demanded, cajoled, but the recruit had a death-grip on the net and wrapped his legs tightly around the cross pole. Sergeant Murphy turned to me.

"Moran, get up there and get him down." My heart stopped. I was just as afraid of heights. "Why me? Send Hunter," I thought. Jim Hunter was a roofer and could have walked up the net with a bundle of shingles on each shoulder. But I knew better than to protest.

I slowly climbed the net without looking down. At the top, I tried to talk him over, but he wouldn't move. I grabbed his legs and pulled them toward me and his body weight forced him over. Now he was on my side, and we climbed down. I could have killed him. To this day, I don't know how I did it.

Each morning after inspection we marched for an hour. Every movement, individual or group, was done with military precision. The class members who had been in the military shone. Under the critical eye of the drill instructor, the few nonmilitary types were quickly discovered. It was easy to be noticed when forty-five people turned left, and one turned right.

The parade field was difficult to march on because of the uneven grass surface. Heels didn't click and bounce off grass as they did on asphalt. Specks of dust swirled up and covered boots with a light brown coating; slight depressions jarred the reaching leg. But the drill instructors were my greatest problem.

There were four. Each had his own unique style, method and rhythm. One instructor's commands were totally unintelligible, and I never knew what he was saying. I constantly got his goat.

"Hold it! Stop! Halt!"

"Moran, don't you understand English!" he bellowed.

I cringed, trying to hide among the pack. Hands on his hips, he continued: "Why don't you listen to the commands and do what you're suppose to, you idiot." Disgusted, he walked back to the side of the column.

"Stand by. *Forwaaaard Maaaarch.*"

But troopers don't march around the Commonwealth in the performance of duty. In the early days, they traveled by horse and motorcycle. By the late thirties, the car had replaced the horse, but the motorcycle lingered despite its danger and obvious shortcomings. Some changes came more slowly than others. The State Police owned over a hundred motorcycles, and until 1970 each recruit class was trained in their use. But the bikes killed more troops than bullets, and many men suffered serious disabling injuries while riding on patrol. We all knew that, but we were thrilled by the power and speed of the large Harley-Davidson machines.

In the middle of motorcycle training, we began another clinical skill—firearms training. While the leaves were losing their color, we marched to the supply depot and received a Smith and Wesson, model 19, six-inch .38 caliber revolver. After we unwrapped the weapon and removed the preservative, we spent hours dry firing at pasted dots on the barracks wall. There was a constant noise of firing pins clicking on empty cylinders.

Finally, we drove to the firing range in Southborough, where we spent many autumn days learning to shoot straight. One of the instructors would drive the large, two-tone blue bus to and from the firing range. We were trained in two courses: marksmanship, which stressed accuracy alone, and combat, which concentrated on speed, accuracy and double action shooting, a new concept in police training at the time. The many hours at the range ended with instruction in the use of the shotgun and .30 caliber rifle.

And then there was time in the classroom doing courses in criminal law, court procedure, evidence, motor vehicle law, policy and procedure, departmental rules and regulations, plus a host of shorter courses. We believed that once we were in the classroom for the day, we were safe—that is, the harassment was minimized if you knew enough not to look for trouble.

I can still remember the military veterans gasping when I corrected Sergeant Marty Murphy concerning the precise location of the rebellion led by Daniel Shays. When I finished telling him that Shays was from Pelham and not Concord and that the armory seized was in Springfield, I quickly found out that I wasn't back in college. Each morning for a week I was asked an obscure question about history. When I failed to answer correctly, I was reminded of my limited intelligence. I got the point. This wasn't college, and I wasn't in charge. This was the State Police and you did what you were told without question or comment.

Sixteen weeks passed quickly. The hot, late-summer sun no longer scorched the parade field and corrugated metal buildings of the academy. We bundled up in thick wool coats and wore gloves during our practice for graduation. Because it was winter, we received our diplomas inside the large Commonwealth Armory in Boston. As our bus plodded along the turnpike we realized this was the last time that we would all be together as a group. Everyone was lost in his own thoughts, concerned, I am sure, about whether or not he would measure up. The usual horseplay was at a minimum.

I reviewed the sixteen weeks. My memories had their share of pain and fear, but I knew the training would pay off. Later in my career I became an instructor myself, and I gave my recruits as good as I had got. There would be plenty of times during my experience on the highways when I would have to rely on the endurance and readiness learned during training.

Two hours later we were making the last return trip to Framingham as the Forty-fifth Recruit Training Troop. We had been sworn in by the governor and given our assignments by the Lieutenant Colonel. We had bullets in our guns and badges on our chests. It was time to put our training into practice. We were troopers.

2. You Can't Always Tell a Good Guy by the Color of His Hat

Hey Sarge, if a guy points a gun at you—is that job stress?

Time: Rookie season
Location: Coastal Route 1
Duty: Padlock patrol

No matter how much the passage of time dulls your memory, certain events in your career or life remain imprinted on your mind. For police officers, performing the varied duties required by direct contact with the public creates an emotional seesaw that constantly shifts back and forth between high drama and deadly boredom. The key events a trooper remembers are usually the ones that contributed to his seasoning: a deed that led to a promotion or an action that pegged him as a veteran. Or it might be the time he was the most scared. You don't forget an incident that could have ended your career just as it was beginning.

Don't think that troopers are involved in gun battles every day. What you see on television doesn't represent police work any more than Dr. Frankenstein represents the entire medical profession. The vast majority of police officers worldwide spend their entire careers without ever drawing or firing their weapons, except at the practice range. But while most cops go through their years on the job without ever firing a shot in anger, or even having a weapon pointed at them, none of us ever forgets that it *can* happen, anytime, anyplace. It's kind of a subliminal thing; part of the job. You don't spend all day dwelling on the possibility of getting shot—you'd never come out of the men's room for cripes sakes—but it's never too far from your mind either. The danger of being killed in the line of duty definitely adds to stress on the job.

Most cases where shots are fired, whether you do the shooting or are being shot at, involve being in the right place at the wrong time. You are there because the job called for you to be there, and you do your job as you've been trained to do it.

On my rookie stint at Topsfield barracks I was assigned to ride shotgun with Trooper Tom Cain. To this day Tom remains in my estimate one of the best cops who ever strapped on a gun. Being under Tom's wing turned out to be the greatest training I could hope for, but at the time I was too indignant at never being allowed to make a decision on my own to appreciate that fact. Tom's job was to teach me, as best he could, the stuff that didn't appear on the academy curriculum. He used a correct, exasperating teaching method: he handled me as if he were dealing with a congenital idiot.

Cain was a classically handsome man of Newfoundland-Irish stock. The son of a Gloucester fisherman, he had served as a paratrooper in Korea and returned to join the State Police. He had been building a reputation as a solid cop ever since.

It was considered a high honor to be broken in by Cain. Even though I resented Cain not giving me more responsibility, especially at first, I realized I was getting good training. Remember that in those days we were required to live in-barracks, getting home only on days off. We worked what amounted to a 104-hour workweek, so I saw a lot of Cain.

Even to the most eager new cop, shaking doors is monotonous work after the first few times, and it is doubly boring on rainy, miserable midnight shifts, popping in and out of the cruiser to inspect the darkened back doors of buildings. Wishing I was home in a nice warm bed, I tried to keep my high-gloss boots out of the puddles. On nights like this even burglars stayed home. The sane ones, anyway. Weekday nights were the worst, with little traffic or late-night activity in this suburban neck of the woods to help the time pass more quickly.

The hours between three and seven in the morning were the toughest for me, when the hands seemed frozen on the clockface. The junior man in the car was always relegated to riding shotgun while the more experienced man drove and made all the decisions. I mean all the decisions—even when we'd stop to use the men's room. We new guys were expected to sit there and act deferential while the senior man revealed valuable inside information—like how to turn a doorknob.

Fortunately for me, Tom Cain was neither boring nor insensitive, but attuned to what a new trooper needed to know. Though impatient to be entrusted with some responsiblity, I was constantly learning. Tom was a stickler for doing the job right. Believing in the famous military dictum *pay attention to detail*, Tom didn't just check the buildings with a history of being left unlocked. He checked every single doorknob on his assigned patrol. The same meticulousness went into every phase of the job. Though my ego twitched, playing second banana, and though my youthful high-spiritedness made me ache to be out and doing more, I was in awe of Cain's patient efficiency.

We'd checked a dozen buildings along the old interstate that night before we pulled in behind the darkened roadside bar. Even though it was a rainy, murky night, Tom wasn't slacking off on me. The rear parking lot was cratered with puddles, and Tom seemed to bounce his cruiser spotlight beam off everyone of them as he searched the dark corners.

The rear door of the roadside lounge was ajar. No cars in sight. My adrenalin started flowing. Was someone hiding inside? Tom and I edged toward the open door. Guns drawn, covering one another, we slid into the blackness of the bar's interior. In the silent storeroom we waited for our eyes to adjust to the lack of light. We hardly breathed, listening for any sound.

Tom whispered, "Someone's in here."

Crouched and silent, straining to see, I wondered how Tom came to that conclusion. Suddenly, from our right, came the crash of breaking glass. Tom and I whirled toward the sound, revolvers pointed, ready to fire.

The barroom cat slunk off, skirting shards of the cocktail glass he'd bumped from the bar. I don't know how many lives that cat had left, but he almost scared me out of my only one. I itched to use up one of his.

We searched the building. There had been a break-in, but the burglar had flown. Tom radioed a report to the barracks asking them to alert the owner and have him come to the scene. I felt bad for the proprietor. After his arrival he wrung his hands pitifully as he surveyed his establishment, finding new cause for distress at every turn.

"They took all the money," he moaned, holding out an empty cashbox. "Kept all my food money in here. Musta got a couple hundred at least. And—jeeze, all my best booze is gone too—cases of it! They musta had a truck!"

"Anything else missing?" Cain asked. I thought I detected a note of sarcasm in my partner's voice.

"Yeah, they got my gun from behind the bar. Revolver, a .22 caliber."

The owner stayed to clean up the mess and secure his building. Tom and I got back on patrol, now doubly alert. I had sensed some antagonism between Tom and the bar-owner, but waited until we'd radioed in our new information and were back rolling again before I said anything.

"You and that bar-owner have some kind of beef in the past, Tom?" I asked, being as diplomatic as I could. I felt sorry for the poor guy that got cleaned out.

"Nothing personal, Dave. It's just that we're always nailing this guy, or others like him, for serving minors or violating the law on the closing hours. He calls that harassment—thinks we should look the other way just because business isn't what it used to be. Same goes for a lot of these roadside joints on Route 1."

We continued patrolling along the coastal route as Tom spoke. The new interstate going north from Boston had taken all the New Hampshire and Maine-bound business away from this scenic old road, and we were alone.

"That's their cop-out song whenever we catch them violating the Alcoholic Beverages Control Laws," Tom continued. " 'We're respectable businessmen, but business is bad, fellas, what else can we do?'—as if that meant that just 'cause sales are slow you can peddle booze to kids or stay open after-hours. Like, long as it's money it's okay," Tom finished angrily.

We continued south through Ipswich and Rowley. The knowledge that someone was out there with a stolen revolver was never far from my thoughts. About four in the morning we approached a sedan pulled off to the side of the highway. Tom rolled the cruiser up behind. The car seemed abandoned.

"Check it out," Tom ordered. "I'll put the plate number over the radio, see if it's stolen."

I approached warily, my flashlight beam playing around the parked car. I saw a man in the front seat. Young-looking, he was lying across the seat, eyes closed as though he'd pulled over to rest after a long drive. I worked the light over him, the seat and the car; nothing seemed amiss.

Nearing the closed window, I could see it was indeed only a kid, seventeen or eighteen years old. Probably snuck a few beers, got woozy driving and pulled over, I thought. I tapped the butt of the flashlight on the windowpane. The kid began to stir.

There was something strange about his eyes. He didn't have that fuzzy, unfocused look of someone just waking up. He seemed to have been lying there waiting for me to go away. Shifting his glance, he refused to make eye contact. But there was still an awareness, a tightening of his features that told me he knew I was there—and that he knew I was a cop. My gut signaled something wasn't kosher here.

I gestured with the flashlight. I wanted him out of the car. Circling carefully I watched his movements like a hawk. As he got into an upright position behind the wheel, his right hand snaked under the seat. Warning bells jangled in my head. No time to call my partner. I ripped open his door, reached into the car and snatched him by the collar. With my other hand I grabbed for his right wrist. Got it. And a good thing, too. His hand had come out from under the seat—full of gun.

I yanked him out of the car. The barrel of his gun kept nosing toward me, despite what I thought was a crushing grip on his wrist. Where the hell was Tom Cain? I bashed the guy's wrist into the doorjamb with all the force I could muster. His gun went bouncing onto the road, skidding through the puddles. Yelping in pain, he aimed a knee at my groin. Twisting, I managed to deflect his knee, catching it instead in a kidney. I stifled his noises by slamming him face-first against the back door. I didn't feel my own pain until later.

Today they'd say I overreacted, but there was no doubt this guy was trying to kill me. Holding him, I pinned his arms behind him. Prisoner thus secure, I looked back to the state car for my experienced partner.

Still busy at the radio, Tom hadn't noticed a thing. I might have worked up resentment toward him, but I realized that I hadn't made a sound to let him know I needed help. Just then, he looked up from the cruiser radio to shout a warning.

"Careful, Dave—that's a stolen. . ." He swallowed the rest. I'll never know whether it was Tom's own instinct for danger or my blanched face, but Cain was out of the cruiser and at my side in half a second.

Handcuffed and confronted by two angry cops, it was time for the young prisoner's own expression to blanch. His cowed demeanor told me he'd heard some horror stories about police brutality and feared he was about to pay the supreme penalty for his foolish act.

"I wasn't gonna shoot ya—honest, I wasn't!"

"Sure, kid, sure," I said, retrieving his handgun from the road. I was glad for the movement now, for the chance to use some of the adrenalin pumping through me.

"Really! I'm only a juvenile—you gotta give me a break!"

Though physically mature, it turned out our prisoner was actually only sixteen years old. A tough kid from the rough, working-class Irish neighborhood of Dorchester, he'd been a chronic troublemaker since childhood. As a juvenile he'd been sentenced to the Youth Service Board, Massachusetts's alternative incarceration for young offenders. He had escaped several days earlier and was on the wanted list.

"Why'd you bolt if your convictions were all juveniles?" I asked. Massachusetts authorities have always tended to treat juvenile offenders extremely leniently.

He didn't seem to get my drift. I reworded the question.

"How much time could you have done for just minor beefs? You were underage, legally."

"They was gonna throw away the key they said. Said I'd *never* be released."

"Who said?"

"Youth Board counsellor."

He named the person who threatened him, the very person charged with his rehabilitation. So much for an enlightened bureaucracy. Or maybe the guy was just tired that day.

Our prisoner admitted taking the gun from the cashbox during the burglary of the bar where Cain and I had almost shot the cat. The back seat of his car held six open bottles of Scotch whisky with the barroom spouts still intact. He had a total of twenty-two dollars on his person, representing what the bar-owner called his two hundred dollars of food money. Even in my inexperience, I saw the big discrepancy in inventories.

The owner was still there when we returned to the bar with the kid handcuffed in the back of the cruiser. He didn't seem very pleased to see us come back with a prisoner and the spouted evidence of a grossly inflated loss report. Tom and I put the six bottles of Scotch on the bar.

"Here's your *cases* of booze," Tom said. "We didn't find any truck."

Then Tom slowly counted out the recovered twenty-two dollars that, while being held at gunpoint, our prisoner, who had nothing to gain by lying, had sworn was all he got out of the cashbox.

"This burglar here says this is all that's left of the several hundred you said was stolen." Tom pointed to the kid. "He already confessed, but maybe he'll explain where he spent it all, or lost it—at three o'clock in the morning."

The owner shrugged, looking for a way out like a kid caught telling a lie.

"Look fellas," he whined, "let's just say you guys never found this stuff. That way I can collect..."

Crimson-faced, Tom Cain grabbed the owner by the shirt, yanking him off the floor.

"You file a false insurance claim, I'll personally sign a complaint against you for insurance fraud," Tom said, shaking the owner for emphasis. "Then, I'll personally escort you to the cell you deserve. You following me?"

The owner nodded feebly. He knew when not to argue. Tom released him and wiped his hands as though he had touched something unclean.

Back outside in the cruiser, Tom squeezed the steering wheel, taking a deep breath. His gaze swung slowly from our prisoner back to the respectable businessman cringing in the barroom doorway.

"Tell ya, Moran...sometimes it's hard to tell which one's the criminal."

Since the time of that case there has been some improvement in the treatment of young offenders, although things still have a long way to go. Virtually all law enforcement people agree with the principle of leniency and rehabilitation, but at the same time they wish the judicial system would recognize and treat repeat offenders differently from first-timers.

But, ironically, the gun-toting kid whom the system had scared into a desperate flight had given me my first taste of action. I didn't like the experience, and I didn't go looking for confrontations like that in the future, but I was glad in a way that it occurred. It was an experience a rookie should learn how to handle, and it wasn't the last time it happened.

3. Breaking In, Breaking Out

Don't we get medals for this?

Time: Rookie year
Location: Seacoast
Duty: Learning from Cain

While I was still going through my breaking-in period I learned what the veteran men on the job thought of my mentor, Tom Cain. Every time I'd be sent to another barracks, some old-timer would invariably ask who was breaking me in. When I answered Cain, at least half of them would try to take credit for breaking *him* in. At last count there were about 150 guys claiming the distinction.

He was still working on me. Now that I had a few weeks in and was used to the deadly heartburn from highway diner coffee, I figured it only right that Cain ease up a little on the gung-ho stuff. At least on a guy like me with all my seasoning. I'd talked to other rookies. They told me about their senior partners letting them catch a few Z's on a dead tour. Putting in over a hundred hours a week, I figured I deserved a break once in a while. I tried it with Cain.

A few times, only.

The first time I tried I had already become resigned to him driving and making all the decisions all night. The only thing going down in our sector that tour was unemployment, so I knew he couldn't complain he needed me. And Cain was definitely the type that let you know where you stood.

Tired, it was only a matter of seconds after settling into my seat and getting comfortable before I began to nod. Not hearing any objection from Cain, I quickly fell into dreamland. And it certainly seemed like a dream when this blinding white light came spearing through my eyelids. Once I realized God wasn't appearing to me in a vision, that the light was coming from somewhere outside my brain, I blinked my sleep-heavy eyes open and into the blinding million-candlepower glare of our cruiser spotlight which Cain had swiveled to the inside of the car and trained on my face.

Because he hadn't said anything, hadn't told me not to snooze, I figured he wasn't much of a diplomat. But I'd play his silly game and let him know I was coming of age as a fellow trooper. I pulled my hat over my eyes to block the light and slouched back down into insolent comfort.

I must have been more tired than I thought. After a few minutes of feigned sleep during which Cain didn't respond verbally as I'd expected, either to chew me out, or joke around, I fell asleep for real again. I can't remember what I dreamed about, but in those days it was probably a dream of being a colonel in charge of the entire state force. The screaming voice that shattered my reverie was like the one you hear in horror movies just before the mummy lunges out from behind the curtain to plunge a dagger into someone's heart.

"Look out!" Cain's terror-filled scream blasted my eardrums.

I jerked up, eyes fright-wide, to see the rear end of a tractor-trailer, crawling at 20 miles per hour, looming larger by the split second as we closed on it at 70. My heart lept into my throat and my kidneys were on their own as I stiffened for the rear-ender I knew we couldn't survive. We roared to within a few feet of the huge truck. Tom's laugh was diabolical as he pulled out to pass and slowed, all in plenty of time. The adrenaline pumping through my system now was superior to any alarm clock, and I knew I'd have no thoughts of sleeping the rest of this tour.

Or any other, with Cain. Working with him, you were as alert at four in the morning on a completely dead tour as you were at midnight on a tour crammed with action. When it came my turn to break people in, I realized the other guys weren't kidding when they called the men their "burden." Squiring around a new chicken just itching to try his wings can bring a lot of grief. Times like that, I appreciated Tom Cain's patience more and forgave him causing me temporary heart stoppage.

That persistent alertness had us checking a roadside rest area one freezing February morning when any sane cop would be cooping somewhere. We were in Georgetown, a sleepy eastern Massachusetts town on Route 95, the major interstate connecting Maine and Florida. Luckily enough I held my tongue when Tom started scouring the Howard Johnson's parking lot, looking over every car.

We came upon two cars parked close together, motors running. The occupants were alseep in both, with all the windows closed, an extremely dangerous practice in winter. Carbon monoxide makes for a super suicide, but every year it also takes a heavy toll in people simply wanting to rest from driving.

Tom and I got out to rouse and warn the occupants. Both cars had out-of-state plates, one New Hampshire, the other North Carolina. Close up, the sleepers had a distinctly seedy look. The southern car had several television sets piled in the back seat. Tom and I exchanged glances. This didn't appear to be the Partridge Family on moving day. We banged on the windows of both cars to rouse them. The look of stark panic on the faces of the occupants when they awoke to see two uniformed troopers standing over them told me our suspicions had a firm basis. I drew my revolver, covering them as they exited the cars.

Tom called in the plates while I had the four people stand close together, hands over their heads. I could tell from their body language, they were getting ready to bolt. They kept shifting from foot to foot and their eyes bounced back and forth between Tom and me as if looking for a chance to pull something. I dashed their budding hopes.

"Anyone moves more'n an inch, I'll blow his head off," I said. The shifting stopped.

The four suspects were hairy hippie-types, all in their late twenties. It looked like I wasn't increasing their respect for authority. Tom Cain drew his revolver as he hurried back from running the license check, so I knew the caution I'd taken wasn't totally inappropriate. He must've heard something on the radio.

Just then another state cruiser pulled up with Troopers Tony Grillo and Bob Woodward arriving as back-ups. Both out-of-state cars had been stolen. After cuffing the four, we put two each in a cruiser, and Woodward and Grillo stood guard while Tom Cain and I searched the stolen cars.

Our longhaired suspects seemed to have been busy. Besides the televisions that were in sight, their car trunks yielded several guns, more televisions and various valuable household articles.

Within two hours of returning to the barracks we had the answers on our prisoners. All four had escaped from the North Carolina State Prison a week earlier. Two had been serving time for one murder and were suspects in another since their escape. The other two were breaking-and-entering artists with lengthy records.

The New Hampshire State Police examined the loot we'd recovered, identifying much of it from a series of house breaks in the Concord area over the previous few days. That was cause enough for us to charge them, rather than just hold them for the North Carolina authorities.

We were short on space at the barracks, so we took them to the Newburyport police station. Newburyport, like Salem, was a famous nineteenth century sailing port that had retained much of its old-time atmosphere and architecture as well as many of the old customs. Tom Cain had many friends there from his lengthy stint in the Topsfield barracks.

One, Town Marshal Sullivan, whose title was a throwback to colonial times, turned out to be one of the most interesting men I've ever met. He was Gary Cooper tall and just as sparing of words. He'd spent his youth before the mast and his vocabulary was full of nautical expressions. Nor was his knowledge limited to the sea. Judges and lawyers often deferred to his experience and wisdom in court, especially in marine matters.

Though we had delivered the prisoners, court wouldn't convene until nine o'clock. Our official shift was finished, but Cain and I, as arresting officers, had to wait for the court to open and appear at the arraignment to charge the suspects formally. If that meant four hours of our own time, it was tough. It was a wonder any of us bothered making arrests under those conditions.

We were having coffee in the guardroom with some of Cain's friends when Marshal Sullivan appeared at the door, finger to his lips, and signaled us to follow him in silence.

Curious, I couldn't resist going with him to a room adjacent to the cell area of the ancient stone station next to the courthouse. Using hand signals, Sullivan bid us wait. We waited. Who were we to argue with Gary Cooper? Eventually our waiting paid off, because through some trick of architecture or air drafts we heard the sounds of conversation from one of the cells carried clearly into our room.

It was quickly apparent that the cell conversation we were overhearing was conducted by the four murderers and thieves we'd brought to Newburyport. We listened to them making detailed plans for grabbing our guns from us in court and breaking out of the courtroom—they even planned how many hostages they'd take.

Marshal Sullivan led us back out to formulate a plan of our own.

"Find that room's pretty useful from time to time," he said. Cain and I were speechless. I guess we were both somewhat in awe of this living legend, but we were also in his jurisdiction, so we let him carry the ball.

"I'll have some of my men in the courtroom when you bring them in," he said, smiling broadly. "We don't want them hauling anchor and raising sail too early, now do we?"

Later, in the heavily guarded courtroom, the fugitives were stunned to see their escape plans foiled before they had a chance to enact them. In addition to the extra armed men visible, any court personnel coming into direct physical contact with them were unarmed, giving them no chance to make a grab. After Tom read the judge the charges against them, he revealed every detail of their plans for a breakout. Judge Kelliher set bail at a hundred thousand cash for each defendant and set a near date for their extradition hearing.

By noontime the scene back at our barracks was chaotic. State police from Massachusetts, New Hampshire and North Carolina, as well as a host of FBI men, were all trying to sort out who belonged to what. They were all making a big deal out of what wanton killers these fugitives had been and how lucky it was that no one was hurt in their apprehension. I tried to convey the impression that a little glory was nice, but Tom and I didn't much care by this time—we were just looking forward to a day off. We'd worked straight through, adrenalin flowing most of the time. We were exhausted but happy.

As we were leaving the station, I have to admit I felt a little pride at the reflected praise we'd received. My shirt was getting a little tight, and I couldn't wait to tell somebody. Sergeant Splaine, our station commander, wished us a good day. I hadn't expected an interview with the governor for this great bust that everybody was so happy about, but I expected a little bit more than "good day" from Splaine.

"Hey Sarge," I quipped, only half in jest. "Think we'll get a department commendation?"

Deadpan, Splaine said, "Hey—arresting criminals is what you get paid for." He sounded bored.

Tom Cain whisked me out. His laugh could be heard across the parking lot.

4. Acceptance

Still no medals.

Location: Topsfield barracks
Time: Rookie season
Duty: Highway patrol

In most states people expect a high level of performance from their troopers. Massachusetts is no exception. Massachusetts troopers are constantly under public scrutiny, performing highly visible duties like airport detail and highway patrol. They also serve as bodyguards to the governor and visiting notables. Even detractors would admit that the sight of a well-buffed, in-shape six-footer in his distinctive gray-blue trooper uniform inspires confidence. Despite the fishbowl atmosphere of their profession, the State Police have long enjoyed a cordial relationship with the general population.

Even before the advent of modern public relations and "image-grooming," state troopers generally received tolerance and respect, if not outright admiration, from the public. In my dreaming days as a teenaged civilian, and later as a recruit in the academy, one of the things that inspired and sustained me was the knowledge that as a uniformed trooper I'd get my measure of respect from the public. I also counted on respect from my fellow troopers. To my naive mind, barracks' camaraderie had a gauzy, cinematic quality. I pictured life after the academy like one of those old buddy movies where all troopers were brothers under the skin and your pals couldn't do enough to help you. I wasn't even close. Being the rookie trooper in the barracks guaranteed me only one thing—no respect.

I don't mean respect wasn't forthcoming from the public. To most people, being a trooper stood for something. People were almost invariably polite and respectful, even to a new guy. About the only people from whom a rookie didn't get even a whisper of understanding or acceptance were veteran troopers and noncommissioned officers. Like college hazing or frat initiation, the breaking-in process facing every rookie, we knew, had some peer harassment. That didn't mean we agreed with it or accepted it with enthusiasm. Breaking-in—the name fit.

Graduation from the academy dressed you up in a fancy uniform and put live rounds in your revolver, but acceptance by your working peers came the old-fashioned way. You had to earn it. That took time, but even with time it only came grudgingly from the older troopers.

There's no way to predict what will win acceptance for a rookie. It could be an important arrest; it could be the first time he covers tracks for a veteran; or it might be something as insignificant as the right wisecrack at the right time. But sooner or later a man will cross over an invisible line into acceptance. The trooper that doesn't had better request a transfer.

There was certainly no welcoming committee when I arrived at my first barracks assignment out of the academy. The desk sergeant gave me the distinct impression that if he'd had anything to say about it, he'd send me back for retraining. The other noncoms barely acknowledged my existence, examining me as if I were a strange laboratory specimen. My fellow unranked troopers simply ignored me. It was as if I was a kid in Springfield again, suffering from the chicken pox, with the kids of the neighborhood avoiding my house like the plague.

That early job isolation was intensified by the fact that back then, married or not, troopers on duty were required to eat and sleep at their barracks. We got one day off in four. Married men had to spend 104 hours per week away from the family. If you weren't fitting tight with anyone at the barracks, it could seem like a long road between days off.

But at some point in the breaking-in, human nature eventually asserted itself and overcame the traditional hard-assed attitude. It was never too long before abrasive lectures on the virtue of being seen and not heard gave way to good-natured abuse. I think the promise of revenge kept a lot of us new guys hanging in there, secure in the knowledge that someday it'd be our turn.

During all this internal stuff, we were also expected to perform our regular duties in an exemplary manner. In among the progressively more challenging duties of the rookie was that one incident that would win acceptance for him. He had to be ready. For me, that incident came on a lonely interstate, when I was finally out on my own.

Before and after the daily commuter rushes, our highways become less frenetic, and more manageable for the trooper. During these periods of mostly routine commercial traffic, patterns are somewhat predictable. These lulls enable troopers on patrol time to observe individual cars more closely and focus on stopping vehicles that commit violations. Some troopers say these are the times when they get to test their criminal-hunting instincts. After some time on highway patrol, certain troopers develop a sixth sense, an almost psychic instinct for stopping otherwise perfectly normal-looking cars that are, indeed, somehow in violation. Because the feeling is instinctual, the troopers can't explain it themselves, but either the targeted driver or his vehicle gives off discernible, negative vibes to the trooper.

Some troopers have an almost unerring instinct for stopping cars that contain dope. Some, for stolen property. Others just have a knack for stopping the right car. The car may not be speeding; it may not have any mechanical violations like missing headlights—but while the trooper's checking the vehicle, a computer run on the license and registration invariably turns up something suspect. The driver owes a pile of parking tickets, or he's wanted for child support in Vermont. Or he may have killed someone once...

As much as I admired and respected Tom Cain, it felt good to be out from under his wing. Always a self-starter, I liked being in the cruiser by myself, responsible for my own decisions. I was patrolling the interstate when Florida plates sent a signal to my instincts. In those days, out-of-state plates were reason enough to ask a few questions and pull a routine check. I signaled the driver to pull over into the breakdown lane.

"License and registration please, sir?" I asked, approaching the driver from the rear. He had the hail-fellow, flashy look of an over-the-road salesman. "Sorry, officer. Don't seem to have them with me," he said casually.

That the driver didn't have a license to operate a motor vehicle confirmed my hunch for stopping him and gave me sufficient cause to do a more thorough check. I had him get out of his car, frisking him with my eyes.

"Name?"

"William Breen."

"You want to come with me, Mr. Breen?"

I had him sit with me in the cruiser, guarding against him running away and keeping him close by so that I could pursue my own questions during his license check. I radioed headquarters in Boston for a check on the Florida plates and requested they do a "missing and wanted" on Breen.

In precomputer days, these types of queries were done by hand, and the response time was correspondingly slower, depending where you were geographically and whether your radio had sufficient range to reach General Headquarters in Boston. If not, your messages and requests had to be routed to Framingham barracks, where a dispatcher relayed your request by teletype. Requested information was returned the same way. It often happened that when you called in a request, the teletype was already busy sending or receiving administrative volume, or dealing with another trooper. You just had to wait your turn. And, given the human element, some troopers got on better with the office personnel at HQ. They would naturally get priority handling while others twiddled their thumbs. Sometimes it meant a long wait. My request on Breen was taking a long time. I was being routed through Framingham, and, as a rookie, I couldn't pull any strings.

The precomputer era was also pre-Miranda. The U.S. Supreme Court hadn't yet handed down the ruling requiring the reading of rights to a suspect. Don't get me wrong—I'm in favor of anything advancing human rights. But before the Miranda ruling law enforcement people depended more on personal questioning skills and an ability to loosen up the criminal or person detained. The idea was to get them to volunteer information that might otherwise take forever to arrive via teletype. Waiting while overworked dispatchers and clerks hand-searched paper files for the names of wanted persons could take a long time. The most successful cops were the ones who could establish an instant rapport and get suspects to open up.

Waiting for Boston HQ to get back to me, I used all my newly learned skills on this guy Breen, hoping he would reveal something to justify my hunch, especially the kind of information that isn't recorded in official files. And William Breen seemed almost too eager to talk. He seemed inordinately eager to please me, something I took as a warning signal.

I sensed he had something to hide. There was more going on here than met my eye. For one thing, the guy didn't sweat at all getting stopped without a license. That was one violation I thought everyone worried about. This suspect was so cool I began thinking he'd been the governor's old roommate in college. Or, perhaps, guilty of something far more serious than a license violation, he was chattering to keep me distracted and deflect me from finding out the truth.

Breen kept up a breezy stream of conversation, as if we were two old pals or fellow commuters meeting at the train station after a busy day in the stock market.

"Used to be a police officer myself," he said. "Somerville force. Quit 'cause of the dough. Live in Florida now, working construction."

"What brought you back up north, Bill?"

"Funeral. Buddy of mine, Russ Nicholson. Died."

Russ Nicholson? I couldn't believe it. Nicholson was a local bad guy—real bad. And this yapper with no legal papers, someone I'd never heard of before, was calling Russ Nicholson a buddy. I knew I had to keep this guy talking. I felt sure HQ would come back with something major, and criminal, on Breen. Anyone connected with Russ Nicholson in any way was suspect in my book.

Nicholson was a rogue cop who had formerly served with the Metropolitan District Police and, as the song goes, "fallen in with evil companions." Eventually he left the police force. His alleged new employers, the mob, ultimately found reason to fault his work and terminated his employment by way of several bullets to the head.

Troopers from Topsfield barracks had found Russ Nicholson's body, stuffed in the trunk of an abandoned car, less than a mile from their station. They took it as a personal affront, and they were extremely anxious to nail the killer. Nicholson's status as an ex-cop, the style of his slaying and the proximity of the corpse to the barracks seemed to make this dumping a macabre message from the mob to the staties.

The gruesome murder had all the earmarks of a contract hit. The police figured it an outside, foreign-contract job because it fit perfectly the MO for that type of gangland slaying. A killer from a distant place is imported for one quick job, then spirited out of town, leaving local police little to work with. Also, because the victims are usually unsavory mob figures, there is little public enthusiasm for the apprehension of the hit man. In the Nicholson case, where the victim had also violated public trust, there was even less sympathy.

Nonetheless, it was murder. And of a particularly brutal type. Nicholson's mutilated corpse had obviously suffered at the hands of someone with a cruel and sadistic twist. And in the meantime, Breen, another ex-cop gone sour, was telling me that he was only up from Florida for the funeral of an old friend. Sure. It's not totally unlike mob arrogance to weep copious tears over the casket of a man they'd ordered assassinated.

Half an hour had passed since my request to HQ, and there was still no reply. How long could I hold this guy? Luckily, Breen was a compulsive talker. I'd throw in a question once in a while to prime the pump, and Breen gushed a steady stream of words. Some of what he spewed out was nothing more than small talk; some of it simply New England crime gossip. But a lot of his babble concerned criminal cases past and present that I was sure our detectives would appreciate some inside intelligence on. Breen mentioned a few things about important cases that I knew were still unsolved. I tried to get him to elaborate, setting the information firmly in my mind without letting on to him that I was overly interested.

Breen seemed especially knowledgeable concering the bloody, headline-grabbing feud between the Winter Hill mob of Somerville and the McLaughlin brothers gang from Charlestown. At the time I stopped Breen, the war had been raging for over a year, and dead gangsters were springing up around Boston like poison mushrooms after a rain.

The feud had started at Salisbury Beach, a seaside resort north of Boston, during the Labor Day weekend of 1961. Feelings grew hot between one Buddy MacLean of the Winter Hill mob and George, one of the McLaughlin brothers. George was paying too much attention to a lady already spoken for by a member of MacLean's mob. The feud spread into their respective gangs and quickly escalated to an all-out, public-be-damned shoot'm up. The press dubbed it an Irish Gang War. The gangs displayed total disregard for the civilian population, and many of the shootouts took place on busy public streets.

Breen seemed to enjoy gossiping about all phases of mob activity, as only an insider could. He dropped names like a social climber, supplying what sounded to me like secret information on organized crime in Boston. Mind you, he wasn't totally deranged. With no witnesses to our chat, he could later deny everything he said. Except for my occasional question, he talked nonstop for forty-five minutes before gesturing to my cruiser shortwave.

"Much longer, you think?" he asked.

I tried every stall I could think of, including blaming atmospheric conditions. Nothing had come back from HQ that I could hold Breen on. For that matter, nothing had come back from HQ period. Knowing my problem, Breen pressed me for an answer.

"Still nothin', huh?" What he meant was, *either let me go or come up with some charges.* He had me. With no response from HQ in all this time, if I detained him still longer, he could bring suit for false arrest. Proving that my fledgling instincts were right didn't seem worth jeopardizing my budding career just then. I wrote Breen up for the license violation and reluctantly let him go.

I resumed patrol. I wasn't seeing much, except red. My mind was busy inventing new cures for the bureaucracy that, though necessary to our function, often seemed designed to impede the officer on the line from performing his job properly.

A full hour after I'd let Breen go, an anxious Framingham HQ came over the air.

"Cruiser 64, you still got that subject stopped?"

"Let him go a while back," I answered. Still the raw rookie, I couldn't just blurt out "I told you so," but I didn't try to conceal the sarcasm in my voice. "Guy said he was late for a funeral."

HQ sputtered for a bit, but they could hardly reprimand me. I'd done everything by the book. It turned out that Breen was officially wanted only for a minor motor vehicle violation at the time. If he'd been held up much longer than I had, a smart lawyer could've cleaned our clocks, even in those days before the Miranda ruling. But there was no guarantee one of our detectives wouldn't have tried if they could've gotten their hands on him.

Later that night I discovered that a lot of people had good reason to question Breen on matters other than minor traffic beefs.

Because of space restrictions, the boots at Topsfield barracks were consigned to bunks in the attic of the old building. These quarters didn't afford even a hint of privacy, but they were clean and roomy. Unfortunately, if you were a light sleeper, you were jolted awake every time anyone put on the communal overhead lights strung from the rafters. I'd been there long enough not to be shocked when the light's glare dragged me from dreamland. What did surprise me was the crowd of people that greeted my slow awakening.

Gathered around my bed were a corporal, a sergeant, a detective lieutenant and several well-dressed guys I knew were FBI agents. I blinked to see if J. Edgar Hoover would also materialize—all that brass around my humble cot seemed like a dream. The sergeant broke the silence.

"Sorry to wake you up, kid." It didn't sound like he meant it.

Detective Lieutenant O'Malley sat down on the edge of my bunk. Although respected as an intelligent and able investigator by the veterans, O'Malley was a terror to the new troops, especially me. He was surly, and as short of temper as he was of stature.

"Hi, Dave. Hope we didn't scare you with this crowd," O'Malley said, his voice syrupy.

Usually the butt of his moods, I couldn't believe O'Malley was being human. He was talking to me like a father.

"These federal gentlemen would like to talk to you about the guy you stopped today, Breen?"

I could tell from O'Malley's ingratiating manner and the anxious looks he cast toward the "federal gentlemen" that either O'Malley owed some favors, or retaining his present status depended somehow on what information I was willing to share with the FBI.

Needless to say, I wanted to do anything in my power to help nail someone like Breen. But I also wanted O'Malley to think I was doing it solely for his benefit and for the good of the troop. The object of everyone's attention, I felt a pleasant surge of power as I rose slowly from my bunk. I offered to help. The FBI, I found out, wanted to talk to Breen about the circumstances surrounding Nicholson's death. They had been looking for him at the same time I was radioing HQ and getting the long-delayed answer about the minor traffic violation.

The federal gentlemen, as well as my own people, were amazed that Breen had gabbed so long with a mere rookie. They wanted to know everything he said. They found it difficult to accept that a novice had enough cop sense to try to detain Breen until something could be found on him, even though the attempt failed.

I was the center of attention. The FBI wanted to hear even the smallest details over and over again. They were hanging on my every word. It was a heady feeling for a rookie who was just getting used to being ignored. Drawing up a chair, I rubbed the sleep from my eyes and started telling war stories about organized crime in New England, as related by Bill Breen.

I didn't really embellish much, but I couldn't resist imparting the crime intelligence in such a way that it was obvious that the volume of information was due mainly to my superb interrogation skills and diplomatic handling of Breen. It was also obvious from the way the brass and my barracksmates pulled up chairs, straining to hear my every word, that I'd finished breaking in.

I wasn't a boot any longer.

5. Murder, He Wrote

Something strange might have happened...

Time: November, 1963
Location: Moneyed North Shore suburb of Boston
Duty: Routine patrol and investigation

The butt of my long-barrelled .38 caliber pistol dug into my side. I kept one eye on the road as I adjusted the heavy weapon for what seemed like the thousandth time that tour. I was still new enough to sweat the uniform infraction, so I wasn't about to un-buckle that heavy leather Sam Browne belt—despite the fact that it weighed around seven pounds with the six-inch service issue Smith and Wesson, steel hand-cuffs and twenty-four spare rounds of am-munition. The weapon alone weighed about three pounds. I pulled over and dismounted to fix the damn belt. I was south of the bar-racks, thinking about calling in a code four and taking a quick break for coffee, when my radio squawked. I heard my designa-tion over the static burst, followed by orders to call the station by phone. The order was not an unusual signal, but a way of convey-ing a personal message or information better left off the airwaves.

Ralph Splaine was the sergeant on duty when I called in. Splaine ordered me to investigate a possible incident at a local residence, the mansion of one of the North Shore elite. Only later did I learn that the mansion belonged to the son of the fabled Lady Astor. And that it held the principals involved in my first murder case.

"Hey kid," Splaine began.

I may not have been a boot any longer, but I was still at the bot-tom of the roster of twenty-one troopers assigned to the Topsfield barracks.

"Get over to the Shaw place, next door to General Patton's estate. See what's going on. The guy's doctor called from Boston. He's worried about him."

I held my questions and rolled on the call. Looking back now at the Agassiz Shaw case from the vantage point of over twenty years experience and the advent of computerized police work, I have to smile. The reason I got the call on that case was that in those days the local police department was a one-man operation. He liked to wrap things up by six o'clock on weeknights, leaving any after-dark crime for the troopers.

Rolling the cruiser up the Shaw driveway, my first impression was that the white, wood-framed structure seemed considerably less imposing than neighboring estates in the area. An ancient red barn sat behind the main house. I parked my cruiser near the rear door, then knocked and banged on all doors front and back. Receiving no response, I let myself in through the kitchen door, shouting loudly, "State Police—anyone home?" Nothing.

The kitchen was eerily quiet, quiet enough for my imagination to conjure up Alfred Hitchcock's knife-wielding *Psycho* character lunging at me from behind a closed door or around the next corner. I didn't let that thought brew too long.

I began to look around the first floor of the house, letting out an occasional "anyone home?" as I went. I knew I'd be embarrassed if I came across the inhabitants sleeping or making love, not having heard the Boston doctor's call. Leaving the kitchen I spotted a large card with a bunch of names on it next to the wall telephone.

At this time I didn't know I was in the home of Louis Agassiz Shaw, socialite son of Lady Astor. Graduate of Harvard, former champion collegiate boxer, renowned amateur scholar, Shaw took his exalted position in society very seriously. The card I noticed near the phone was a roster of sorts, a twenty-by-thirty-inch list of names published by the Social Register, the four hundred families deemed socially acceptable and worthy of note. I later learned that Shaw had issued strict instructions to his house servants and other estate employees to accept calls only from callers bearing names on that list.

After a thorough, fruitless check of the first floor, I used the kitchen phone to report to Splaine. The dispatcher sounded concerned. He'd received yet another call from Shaw's alarmed Boston physician.

"Take another look around kid—the doctor says Shaw called him from the mansion less than an hour ago. He's afraid something strange might have happened."

I did a quick grounds search, turning up nothing exceptional outside, either. The barn provided my first clue into the strange goings-on, although I didn't recognize it as a clue right then. In the barn sat a showroom-condition Cadillac sedan, gleaming and dentless although it was one of the finned models dating back to the Korean War era. Checking the odometer I found the reason why. The car had only thirty-five hundred miles on it—thirty-five hundred in more than ten years! At the time it was just part of a growing mystery. I went inside to check out the second floor.

The wide double straircase looked like something out of the movies, with curved, polished railings. On opposite walls hung large, expensively framed paintings. Great copies, I thought. I was so engrossed in the artwork I almost stumbled over the body.

"Jesus Christ!" my brain registered. "She's been strangled!"

A motherly woman of about sixty was staring right up at me, wide-eyed, mouth gaping. I saw immediately she'd been choked to death. It may have been my first dead body, but you didn't need four years of medical school to recognize that type of violent death.

I drew my pistol. Heart pounding, I started down the hallway past the body. It was as if each one of my senses had become supersharp. I felt a heightened sense of hearing, smell and touch. Some instinct told me the murderer was still in the house. One thing was for sure—the doctor who called the barracks had been correct to assume all was not normal at the Shaw residence.

I didn't know who the dead woman was, but I half-expected to find the owner dead next, the victim of an art heist or kidnap attempt gone wrong. The visible facts disputed that, however. The downstairs and what I'd seen so far of that hallway were unransacked, showed no signs of struggle or anything out of the ordinary. Needless to say, going down that hallway my imagination was working overtime. It took all the discipline I could muster to let my training take effect.

Gun extended, I checked each bedroom along the hallway, making a circuit that brought me back to the body near the top of the stairway. And the last bedroom. Something told me that if I was going to find anything, this room was where it would be. I opened the last door with even more caution than the others. I was ready to blast anything that moved.

Behind the door was another door. The second door loomed wider and heavier than the first. I'd never seen a door behind a door except in a Frankenstein movie. I didn't dwell on that for long, either.

I pushed through the second door. Entering a long, narrow, well-lighted room, I realized why the double doors. A sound baffle. The room was a library. Stacks of books wall-to-wall and floor-to-ceiling. Books.

And a man in an armchair staring at me.

At the opposite end of the room was a fiftyish guy seated calmly in a stuffed chair. I figured it had to be the owner, Shaw. Amazingly, he showed no observable reaction to a state trooper stalking into his study with a long-barrelled thirty-eight for a calling card. What bothered me even more was his calm demeanor when a dead body lay outside his door.

Then I noticed he was sitting with a laprobe over his legs and his hands out of sight under the robe. Given what I'd found in the hallway, I automatically assumed he had a weapon. Following the book, I leveled my gun on him. It wouldn't have taken too belligerent a move under the robe for me to react. Finally, he acknowledged my arrival. But his look was as if I'd just tracked mud on his Persian carpet.

"And just who might you be?" His tone suggested that I'd also interrupted his morning meditation.

"State Police," I responded automatically. Taking a long shot, I blurted, "Why'd you kill her?"

"She was bothering me. Made too much noise!" he answered sedately. "I *told* her to stop."

He spoke as if he were trying to be very patient with me. By this time I was questioning my own mental condition. Nonetheless, I kept my gun on him.

"Hands out from under the blanket—slowly," I ordered.

He didn't move a muscle. Instead, it was as if the light went out behind his eyes at the same time his focus mechanism quit. He began to mumble. He appeared delusional. Keeping my gun trained on him, I moved quickly, whipping the blanket off his lap.

He was holding a book.

Once I was certain he was unarmed, the immediate threat was over. I sensed this guy was beyond being a threat to anyone else. I holstered my gun and arranged the laprobe around him again. Our peaceful tableau was abruptly shattered by the pounding boots of two back-up troopers Splaine had sent to find out why I'd been so long calling in.

The doc had been right, after all. Something strange had definitely happened. Following procedure, I arrested the socialite and escorted him back to the lockup. At the barracks, the detective lieutenant explained to a seemingly rational Shaw, that he would have to appear in the Salem District Court for arraignment in the morning. The prisoner was exceedingly pleasant and cooperative.

"Fine," he agreed. "My chauffeur will drive me over. What time am I to appear?

Either he was beyond help or he was the coolest prisoner ever held in Topsfield barracks. The lieutenant explained as politely as he could to Shaw that he was being held for murder. Then he signaled discreetly to the officers.

"Perhaps it would be best if Mr. Shaw remained our guest for the evening."

The next day the detective lieutenant ordered me back to the estate and the crime scene to construct diagrams for possible trial use. Climbing that staircase, I immediately saw that the two paintings that so impressed me the day before were missing from the wall. When I finished at the crime scene, I called the prestigious Boston law firm that handled the family's affairs. I reported the disappearance of the two paintings I'd noticed earlier, hanging by the staircase.

"Which paintings?" I was asked, as if everybody had several. I described the two.

"Oh, those," the law clerk answered. "We removed those paintings this afternoon—placed them temporarily with the Boston Museum of Fine Arts. For safekeeping. Originals—they're priceless, you know.

I returned to the barracks. About three in the morning Donald MacDonald, the desk officer, woke me asking that I follow him downstairs to the lockup to see what was happening with their prisoner.

"You studied some French, maybe you can figure out what tongue your prisoner's babblin' in. It's no language I ever heard."

Mystified, I followed MacDonald. After the events of the day I didn't think there were any surprises left, until we got downstairs. Shaw stood in the far corner of his cell, gesticulating wildly as if he were sprinkling holy water. Louis Agassiz Shaw, product of proud Yankee Protestant stock, the ultimate WASP, was reciting the entire litany of the Roman Catholic mass—in Latin!

The next day Judge Harrington ordered a temporary commitment to Danvers State Hosptial for psychiatric evaluation. Shaw never came out to stand trial for murder.

6. The Clark Case

Crime pays, but not as it should.

Time: Mid-1960s
Location: Pioneer Valley
Duty: Area patrol

Of all state police assignments in Massachusetts, those in the rural, western part of the state present the largest geographical area to cover. Headquartered in Northhampton, near the center of the state, Troop B has jurisdiction over an area stretching all the way to Goshen and the New York state border. B Troopers enjoy some exceptionally interesting assignments because, contained within their patrol area, are sectors as diverse as any metropolitan area, as well as interstate highways, several college communities and the many isolated farms of the Pioneer Valley.

Troop B has thirty-six hundred square miles to cover. During the time I was assigned to Troop B there were fifteen towns too small to support their own police departments. Except for the occasional elected town constable, these towns relied solely on the State Police for law and order. From the centrally located barracks, a trooper could drive for an hour in any direction of the compass before reaching the patrol terminus. That may not seem astounding to someone from Montana, but it is quite remarkable in the crowded, industrial Northeast.

Western Massachusetts is a scenic delight, a magnet to tourists. Even to a jaded New England native, fall in the Berkshire foothills is an incredible experience. Nature presents an annual magic lantern show, splashing colors around the hillsides as long as the leaves of oak and maple, elm and aspen cling to their branches. The crisp, clean air spreads a heady scent of pine and red apples.

But fall also brings thousands of young students back to the area's colleges, to Smith, the University of Massachusetts, Mt. Holyoke and Amherst, bringing with them the quickness of the season and the high of Saturday-afternoon football, and geometrically increasing the workload of state police serving the area. The calls I dreaded most were the ones that came on Saturday nights after a college game, when you knew the kids were celebrating, drinking and driving. As long as young people continue to mix booze, or any other drug, with driving, there will always be tragedy and death included in college weekends. The tragic element is magnified when there are students from four colleges within the patrol boundaries, plus weekend visitors.

The law of averages supplies a steady stream of kids ready to defy the odds against becoming traffic statistics. No one thinks it can happen to him. The worst shame is they're mostly dynamite kids, kids newly away from parental restrictions, drinking just to be part of the crowd or just having a few to celebrate the college game. I wasn't much older than many of them when I was stationed in Troop B. I really hated those accident calls.

Eerie scenes of twisted, smoking wreckage that we've all seen far too many times on television...dripping antifreeze and hot, slimy oil escaping from engine blocks...odd auto parts scattered along the roadway...the moans and cries of injured people...silent groups of hushed survivors too horrified to speak above a whisper, aware of spectator luck, aware that for them the only consequence beyond a nightmare memory would be the party they missed or tomorrow's hangover. I would have given anything not to have to answer those calls.

But even though auto accidents were commonplace in western Massachusetts back then, violent crime was almost unheard of. The astronomical escalation of drug-related crime and violence that was swamping the cities hadn't yet reached the Berkshires. Lately we've become so inured to violent crime that it seems improbable, but in the sixties armed robbery was rare news, at least in rural America.

The night the message that marked the beginning of the Clark case came over the radio, my first reaction was simply relief that it wasn't a summons to another accident scene involving college kids. I was cruising Route 5 around Whately when the call came, routing me to Plainfield.

"Report of prowlers. Meet Constable Harris at the Clark place."

"501, received. Moving." I swung the cruiser around and headed across country on rarely used back roads toward Route 116 and Plainfield.

The Clark place belonged to Bob Clark, a local character who sold car and truck tires from the barn of his ancestral farm in Plainfield. Old Bob was an original Yankee eccentric. To be deemed authentically eccentric in that neck of the woods, when competing with so many of what are charitably titled hardy individualists, took some doing. But Bob was a very interesting character.

In the early 1920s, about the time it became obvious the automobile wasn't just a flash in the pan, Bob Clark began selling tires out of his barn in Plainfield. In his typically direct fashion, Clark personally visited the owners of fledgling rubber tire manufacturing companies in Akron and Indianapolis, bypassing their New England sales reps and the middleman profits as well. His thinking was far enough ahead of his time that in some cases Clark established himself as a cash customer at the factories before they'd even formed a regular sales force. Because of this early and direct association with the manufacturers, he formed deals that latecomers, even giant wholesale distributors, couldn't obtain. In addition to his favored-party status, Bob Clark had no overhead to pay. His barn had been paid off for generations, and he was his only employee. Nor did he believe in advertising, except by word of mouth.

The system worked. Forty years later, Bob Clark was still selling thousands of tires annually to customers who came from all over New England and upstate New York. He defied economic theories, disdained modern marketing techniques, laughed at media hype and became a huge success. Bob Clark didn't even own a cash register. All he had was a slew of customers and a barn full of tires.

Whipping the heavy cruiser down those dirt roads, I felt a twinge of worry for old man Clark. The dispatcher had told me to meet Constable Harris, the elected local watchdog, at the scene.

That probably meant that whatever had taken place was more than Harris could handle. Theoretically, that could mean anything beyond a treed cat. But the dispatcher had also said prowlers, and it was part of local mythology that Bob Clark kept a lot of cash on hand. And owned no alarm system. I considered what a job professional criminals could do with a set-up like that. I only hoped that if it happened someday, they wouldn't kill Bob doing it.

If Bob had to make change, he'd slip the padlock off the rear door of the house attached to the barn, disappear for a minute or two, then reappear with the correct bills. I'd observed his method myself and warned him about it. Clark didn't take easily to interference—and for Bob, interference was any suggestion he didn't agree with.

Bob Clark had come the closest of anyone I ever met to stopping change. He seemed oblivious to it. A confirmed bachelor, Bob had lived completely alone since the passing on of both his mother and sister back in the 1930s. Although he had no control over his body's aging process, Clark resisted other external change by controlling his immediate environment. Virtually nothing new had come into his house during this century—definitely nothing since the death of his mother and sister. He still used the outhouse constructed with the farm. He still dressed in early Sears Appalachia. He wore high-top laced boots, and Haystack Calhoun overalls over a flannel workshirt. No one in Plainfield had ever seen him dressed in anything different. Bob's teeth had fallen out about the time the Japanese bombed Pearl Harbor, but he couldn't be convinced to replace them for either health or cosmetic reasons. Bob was one of a kind, an anachronism.

Nearing Plainfield I had a dread premonition that time was finally catching up with Bob Clark. A group of people from town was gathered around Bob's dooryard. News travels fast. I pushed through into the farmhouse kitchen to be greeted by a relieved Constable Harris.

"Whacked 'im on the head," Harris said, reporting the obvious.

Bob Clark slumped mutely in a kitchen chair, eyes shock-glazed. Blood from a head cut had dried in the age lines of his face, giving him a ghoulish, clownlike look. Harris had correctly summoned an ambulance while waiting for my arrival. The attendants bustled around now, preparing Clark for the ride down the mountain to the Cooley Dickenson hospital in Northhampton. Constable Harris rushed to fill me in.

"Whacked 'im on the head," he repeated, ending his brief report of three youthful assailants. "Tied 'im up, took his keys and cash, and left 'im layin' in the garden."

I thanked Harris for his report, then searched Bob Clark's eyes, hoping for a glimmer of confirmation.

"Three of them, Bob?"

"Young guys," Bob agreed, nodding painfully, "Never seen them before though. Not that I know of . . ."

Bob was as short on conversation as he was on bookkeeping procedures. I hated to do it just then, but I had to push ahead— both for a few answers in the investigation, and to establish to my own personal satisfaction whether or not Bob truly failed to recognize his assailants. Witnesses often conveniently forget, fearing the return and revenge of the criminal.

This didn't seem to be the case with Bob. Nonetheless, he still couldn't give much of a description beyond the vague age reference. I'd have a chance to question him again later at the hospital. I signaled the ambulance driver to move out.

"I ain't leavin' my place," Clark balked, trying to rise from the stretcher.

Despite his weakened condition, Bob Clark refused to accept medical help until I'd personally guaranteed the security of his farm while he was in the hospital.

"I'll look after the property, Bob," I promised. "Now, go!"

From the driveway I radioed an interim report into HQ. The small crowd of country neighbors and the curious began to melt away when the ambulance turned a bend in the road. Among the crowd was Bill Jones, the rural delivery mailman who covered this route. Bill hung back as the spectators departed. He motioned me aside, a look of worry clouding his face. Bill didn't beat around the bush.

"Those crooks may've gotten a real bundle, Dave," he said. "Old Bob sometimes kept an awful lot of cash around."

Nothing like rumors of hidden treasure to stir up the nosy, greedy and just plain curious. I pulled Bill out of earshot of the others. He was serious. His revelation wasn't entirely a shock to me. There had always been gossip about a Clark treasure. But this was more than gossip.

Bob Clark hoarding a lot of cash made sense—because of his tire business and his eccentricity. Unfortunately it could also mean I was dealing with professional criminals. I had to know how the mailman knew, then prove or disprove what so far was only speculation.

"Tell just what you know for fact, Bill."

"This may all sound a mite odd."

Almost apologetically, the mailman described how he routinely did more for the people living along his route than simply deliver mail. Often he was company for the lonely, bringing welcome news of local people and events. Sometimes he picked up and delivered prescription medicines for the old and sick. Over the years he and Bob Clark devised a system whereby Bob frequently left large manila envelopes in his mailbox by the side of the road. Making his rounds, Jones would pick up and drop off the envelope for Bob at the Haydenville bank whenever he happened to hit there. On a subsequent trip he'd drop off Bob's deposit slip.

"Big deal, Bill," I interrupted. "Every business makes deposits."

That blew it. The mailman suddenly became reticent. I figured either my tone of voice intimidated him or he too had a case of the witness blues. It took some patient explaining and much quiet listening on my part before I realized neither was true. Bill was afraid for his job.

"They got regulations against goin' above and beyond for your customers, Dave," he said. "The PO don't enforce the rules. They kinda look the other way, until they gotta answer to somebody higher. If they ever found out..."

"I won't use your name in my report, Bill. Finish your story."

Bill sighed resignedly, but went on.

"Other businesses don't make deposits like old Bob," he said. "I figured I was just depositing his checks, maybe a few dollars cash now and then, you know how that goes. Cripes, I been doin' this a long time for Bob. Sometimes I'd be late and keep those deposits overnight at my house. Anyways, not long ago, the teller at the Haydenville bank chewed me out for the way I do business. Me? I says, why? That's how I found out that every one of those envelopes I been luggin' for old Bob contained between twenty and thirty thousand dollars—cash money!"

I was incredulous. "Thirty thousand? Each envelope?"

"Cash," Bill repeated. "Nearly died when I found out, too. That means that when Bob missed me, or forgot one deposit, there could be fifty or sixty thousand dollars sittin' around that house for somebody to pick off."

"Christ."

"Yup. Couldn't convince Bob to change his methods, either. You can bet I don't hold 'em overnight anymore. Never told a soul, 'cept you. 'Fraid of being robbed myself."

Before he left, Bill helped me establish the recent date of Bob Clark's last deposit. Beginning my physical investigation of the crime scene in the garden, I wondered what surprise was coming next.

Finished outside, I re-entered the farmhouse, noting the hasp and padlock on the kitchen door that passed for a security system. The lock looked like it belonged in a Wells Fargo museum. In reality, the lock served only for show because everybody knew Bob Clark's system. Anyone buying tires from him over the years could observe his unchanging habit of unlocking the door, going inside to make change for a bill, then back out, carefully replacing the relic of a lock. It probably seemed secure to old Bob Clark, more naive than most regarding man's inhumanity. But anyone over the age of ten could have foiled his system. Thinking of the thousands of customers Bob'd had during his years in business, I knew there was no shortage of suspects.

When calling in my report to base, I had requested a fingerprint and photo man to go over the scene. I decided to look through the house while waiting. I hid my cruiser behind the barn so as not to attract any curious passers-by.

The farmhouse kitchen was cluttered with piles of small boxes and heaps of junk that should have gone to the dump long ago. Beneath the window was an old soapstone sink complete with pump handle. I worked the handle and drank deeply of the frigid, pure spring water. Opposite the sink sat a cast-iron cookstove, a big old woodburner. I could easily imagine myself sitting in this same kitchen reading about Teddy Roosevelt charging up San Juan Hill.

The dining room table and a highboy in the corner were piled high with cracker boxes. A wooden box that may have held pencils or a loaf of cheese lay open and empty on the floor. I began to figure old Bob for some kind of box nut.

The rest of the house was roughly the same—litter and small boxes. Upstairs, the clothing in the closets and the appointments of all the rooms were at least fifty years past vogue.

Back downstairs in the living room, noticing a dented cracker box on a sidetable, I decided to see if it too was empty, like the one I'd found on the kitchen floor. Careful of prints, I flipped up the lid. My heart almost jumped through my shirt. The box was jammed full of money. I think my breathing stopped while I was staring into that box. Talk about Ritz crackers! Rubberband-tied wads of paper money filled the insides.

I reached for another box and opened it. Same thing. Another. Soon there were fifteen boxes of currency open on the table before me, more money than I'd ever seen in one place. I was reaching for more of those cracker boxes when I heard a noise outside the kitchen door. Were the robbers coming back for the loot they'd missed? They wouldn't have seen my cruiser in behind the barn. There wasn't time to hide the pile of loot. My hand slid to my service revolver.

Crouching, I used the partition between the kitchen and dining room for cover. The doorknob was being turned from the outside. Holster unsnapped, my fingers were curling around the gun butt when a smiling, veteran trooper stepped through the kitchen door.

"Don't shoot, Dave. I'm close to retirement."

Walter Dzenis, a popular trooper and highly respected criminologist, was answering my request for a print and photo man. I breathed a huge sigh of relief.

"Glad it's you, Walter," I said. I led him toward the treasure room. "Hope you like surprises."

I heard his quick intake of breath.

"Holy—" Walter sat down abruptly, shaking his head at the sight of all the money-stuffed boxes.

Dzenis was a local farm boy of Polish descent. After serving with the 353rd Infantry during WWII, he returned to Deerfield, choosing the troopers over trying to scratch a living farming from the rocky soil. Finished with his years on the road, he was now held in high regard by other troopers as a detective and a standup guy. His experience and instincts were always available to the younger guys.

I had the feeling this may have been more money than Walter'd ever seen, too. He took a minute to gather himself.

"What'ya think happened here, kid?" he asked, lighting his ever-present pipe.

I hesitated, aware of Dzenis's awesome reputation. But I couldn't stall forever.

"The victim, Bob Clark, could only tell us that his attackers were young," I said. "I think that we can also add inexperienced, although they obviously knew how Clark ran his business—up to a point. Given their youth and the familiarity with his operation, I would assume they don't live too far away."

Walter said, "What pegs them as inexperienced?"

"They don't seem too thorough on *any* phase of this," I said. "They thought they needed his keys, so they whacked him on the head to get them. A real pro would've cased the job correctly, he'd know a good wind would handle that old lock. Then, after needlessly assaulting Bob, they left him out in the garden instead of bringing him inside where he couldn't be seen from the road or driveway. In here, they could have questioned him at their leisure. But what clinches it for me is all these boxes of money that were left behind. That wasn't on purpose. My guess is that they knew Bob Clark kept *some* money in the house. Cripe, *everyone* seems to know that. I think they got in, got as far as that pencil box I found on the kitchen floor, took only what was in plain sight, then ran."

"Why?"

"Either they thought that was all the loot there was in here or got scared off by a noise or saw someone coming. Inexperienced, jumpy, they took off before finding the rest of Bob's stash."

I scrutinized Walter's face to see if my analysis fit his more experienced deductions. Nothing. He relit his pipe with a practiced lack of expression.

"How much money you calculate they actually got away with?"

His question poked through a cloud of pipe smoke. I didn't have the foggiest. An estimate of the amount stolen was of primary importance in any theft investigation, but I was so caught up in my detection theory that I hadn't thought that far ahead. I must've sounded like a real bozo to a man of Dzenis's experience. Luckily, Walter stopped me before I could admit my ignorance.

"Let's begin by counting up all the money that's left," he suggested. "Gonna have to inventory it all eventually, anyway. Then we'll fill the box from the floor as close to the way old man Clark did as we can, using these others as a guide. That should give us some idea of how much they got away with." Walter grinned, letting me off the hook gently. "Don't feel bad, kid. You would've come up with the same idea sooner or later."

It was becoming apparent why Walter Dzenis was held in such high esteem by my fellow troopers from B barracks.

We began counting Bob Clark's money. An hour and a half later Walter and I were finally nearing the end of our count. I was beginning to understand the expression *filthy lucre*. My hands were grimy from counting and handling the seemingly endless piles of bills. I had the weird though fleeting feeling of not caring if I ever saw paper money again.

In the course of counting, Walter and I discovered a basic system to Bob Clark's apparently haphazard filing method. All dollar bills, fives and tens were stacked together in the same area of the rooms in which they were found. Although those denominations were found together, they were never packed in equal amounts. The amount varied with the size of the box. The larger bills—twenties, fifties and up—were consolidated in separate boxes and kept in a different section. It was like the price of real estate—everything depended on location.

During the count all I could think of was how lousy I was at counting *anything*. Normally, if someone asked me for change of a twenty, I'd have to count it three or four times, and I still wouldn't be certain. Now I had to count—and be right—for this investigation. We both finished counting almost at the same time. Walter reached for his matches.

"How much in your pile, kid?"

I told him my total. He did some adding on paper. I knew from just looking at the stacks of cash that the amount had to be more than the mailman had estimated.

"Totals out to $103,765 even. Agreed?"

Agree? Of course I agreed. Did he think I was going to demand a re-count?

"Sounds right to me," I said. "But why keep it here instead of a bank?"

"People're funny, kid," Walter shrugged. "Maybe later in the investigation you'll come up with a valid reason why Clark hoarded this loot; but don't expect logic when dealing with human beings. Ready to try stuffing the pencil box?"

Carefully, and as closely as we could, we simulated Bob Clark's stacking method with the pencil box. Using bills of smaller denominations, we could stuff in somewhere between $2,000 and $2,500. Our conjecture was that the pencil box most likely held smaller bills because of its general location. Nonetheless, we covered all bases by filling the box with other bills as well. This way, we determined that if the box came from the location containing predominantly larger bills, the amount stolen would be about twenty thousand dollars.

After the count, Walter proceeded to dust other objects for fingerprints and take whatever photos he thought might be needed. I started stacking all the boxes of money in the trunk of my cruiser. I kept imagining a variety of stunned and angry reactions if the thieves ever found out how close they had been to the score of a lifetime.

Midnight rolled around before we finished. I locked up the farm and headed for the barracks. After logging me in from the investigation, the desk sergeant helped me pile the boxes of greenbacks into the safe in the captain's office. Upstairs in my bunk at last, I drifted off, counting green-tinted pictures of Ulysses S. Grant.

At breakfast the next morning, the mess hall buzzed with barracks speculation about the case. My fellow troopers were curious about its unusual aspects, especially the money hoard and the lead character, old Bob Clark. I was in for a dose of good-natured sarcasm about what percent of the Clark loot I'd actually turned in to the safe and how much I'd kept.

Walter Dzenis also caught his share of remarks, particularly about the fortuitous timing of his upcoming retirement. I didn't dare share with Walter my fears of screwing up the count. If there were a discrepancy in the amount, we'd never hear the end of it—even if it was proven to be only an error in counting.

After breakfast, I set out to interview the victim. Northampton's Cooley-Dickenson Hospital was at only a few doors from the home of former President Calvin Coolidge, and in many respects old Bob Clark reminded me of the silent president. Clark typified the taciturn nineteenth century Yankee: hardworking, Godfearing and frugal.

Bob was sitting up in his hospital bed looking pretty chipper despite the bandage around his head. He was cleanshaven for a change. A white hospital gown had replaced the bib overalls. His eyes no longer had the glassy, faraway look of the previous evening.

The attending physician stopped by the room to say Bob could be released as soon as the necessary paperwork was finished. They'd tested Bob for concussion and other head damage, concluding he wouldn't need further in-patient care. When the doctor left, unthanked by his patient, I sat on Bob's bed. I worked up my special interrogation stare, hoping it would intimidate Bob enough to get me some straight answers.

"Found some money in your house, Bob," I said.

Bob inspected the linen of his bedsheet very carefully. I let the silence hang. Bob finally nodded his head affirmatively but continued to avoid my gaze.

I said, "Found over a hundred thousand dollars, all told. In a bunch of boxes."

"That much, eh?" he said. He seemed genuinely surprised only at the amount. That piles of cash were found stored in his house didn't seem to be the issue.

"Did I find all the cash, Bob? Or is there more hidden in the house for crooks to find next time?"

"Dunno."

"You don't know if there's more?"

"Nope."

"Then, how much did you have in the house *before* you were robbed?"

"Dunno," he said.

My impatience broke through. "Jesus Christ, Bob. I mean, you must have some idea. You kept some records for your taxes, you could check those, couldn't you?"

Bob scratched his head. "Tax records?" His voice trailed off.

I gave up. Frustrated at my failure to get through to Bob, I helped him into his old farmer togs, checked us out of the hospital and drove back to the barracks to get some specific orders.

The desk sergeant instructed me to hook up with Lieutenant Jim Molloy after lunch. Lieutenant Molloy would accompany Bob and me, and Bob's money, to the Haydenville bank, where Bob at least had a checking account, the one to which Bill the mailman was making cash deposits. As I was coming to know Bob Clark, I assumed the only reason he bothered to keep even a checking account was that the tire companies in Akron frowned on receiving remittance envelopes stuffed with cash.

Outside the mess hall the sergeant stopped to tell me that our captain was so nervous about the money he'd assigned a trooper full time to babysit the safe whenever he had to be out of his office. I invited Bob Clark to break bread with the troops and steered him to one of the smaller tables in the mess hall. My barracksmates weren't showing much class. The noise level in the mess hall suddenly dropped fifty decibels as nearly everyone stopped jabbering to stare at Bob. Admittedly it was a bit out of the usual to have a civilian guest in our dining room, but by then everyone had heard the story of Bob's hoarded money. I can't fault them entirely. How many of us have ever been face to face with someone with a seemingly total disregard for a hundred thousand dollars?

Doubtless Bob's hokey appearance caused some of the attention, too. Toothless, anachronistic in his overalls and high-top shoes, old Bob placidly ate his lunch, oblivious of the ruckus he was causing. He seemed particularly delighted that the meal was free.

When we arrived at the bank, Lieutenant Molloy requested to see the president. The bank employees were eyeing our trio closely, and I can't say I blamed them. We must have presented a rare sight in the carpeted reception area. In his dapper civilian business suit Jim Molloy could have been a banker himself. I wore my trooper uniform, and Bob looked like an aging Haystack Calhoun. All three of us stood waiting, arms piled high with cracker boxes as if we were selling girl scout cookies.

Eventually we were turned over to the care of a young vice-president who ushered us into a private counting room. I spent some time explaining the situation, but the vice-president still went a little bugeyed when we dumped the contents of the cracker boxes onto the counting table. It didn't take him long to recover skills learned in his teller days. What had taken Dzenis and I several hours to count the previous night, he accomplished in under an hour.

"Done," he said, totaling up. I crossed my fingers and prayed our tallies agreed. "Exactly $103,765."

I breathed again. I could just imagine how the other state cops would've construed a miscount. They'd let me forget...about ten years after retirement. That is, if I got a pension.

Now that he had the total, the banker tried sweet reason with Bob to get him to deposit his money in the bank, preferably in a savings account. Under the banking laws of the time, the bank was not required to pay interest on money in checking accounts. What money Bob Clark did have under deposit was in a checking account to pay for his tires. The banker even used the prestige of the FDIC to persuade Bob.

"In addition to being interest-bearing, these accounts are also insured for up to ten thousand dollars by the federal government," he said.

Lieutenant Molloy and I added whatever credibility we had with Bob to the banker's arguments about interest and safety. We nodded our heads and smiled like baboons. This wasn't entirely unselfish on my part. I'd have a lot less headaches in Plainfield if Bob could be persuaded to use bank vaults instead of cracker boxes for his money.

The banker wrapped up his sales pitch.

"Now, Mr. Clark—how much would you like to deposit in one of our safe, secure, interest-bearing savings accounts?"

Bob shrugged. "Government insures my money up to ten thousand?" he asked.

I thought, he's finally seeing the light; I'll be able to sleep at night knowing there's not a line of crooks waiting to knock him off. The banker nodded his agreement, pushing some account forms toward Bob. Bob smiled.

"I'll go the whole ten thousand then," he said.

Sudden silence reigned in the counting room. Lieutenant Molloy was dumbfounded. I was frustrated that Bob would bank only a small fraction of his fortune, but I sensed his intractability. Bob Clark would not listen to logic. He insisted we take him back to his farm with the rest of his stash unbanked. He trusted the banks less than his cracker boxes.

During the next several weeks I was assigned full time to the Clark case. Armed with Bob's rudimentary customer file I traveled around New England. The case took me to many small towns in New Hampshire and Vermont. Because he relied on word of mouth rather than advertising, the vast majority of Bob's customers were rural folk. One small town had dealt with Bob Clark for so long and enjoyed his discounts so much that each year they'd send a truck down to pick up a tire order for the whole town. I met a lot of people who thought very highly of old Bob on those travels, but no serious suspects.

At one point, I did get excited over two prime suspects whom Bob eventually remembered harassing him the day of the robbery. The pair had been around the barn long enough to case his operation during the course of giving Bob a decidedly difficult time over tire prices. They only left when he threatened to call the law. Fortunately for the investigation, Bob had a habit of writing down the license plate numbers of his customers. I say fortunately, because he'd naively accepted their names as Homer and Jethro.

I caught up with the pair in Adams, Massachusetts. Hard drinkers, they were bullies when loaded; rousting old Bob was their idea of amusement. I had already established to my own satisfaction that this pair couldn't have been back in Plainfield at the time of the robbery, but I didn't let them know they were off the hook. After my interrogation, I doubted they'd be bugging any old men for a while.

I chased other leads around the surrounding towns and even out to remote logging camps but still came up empty. The theft of money didn't bother me so much as the callous and needless pistol-whipping of old Bob Clark. I hate to see anyone physically abused, but Bob seemed especially vulnerable because of his touching capacity for trust. Maybe I also yearned for an era when people could trust their neighbors and leave their doors unlocked. Whatever the case, I wanted the guys who hurt Bob.

In time I had a decent handle on some young hoods from a neighboring town. While doing the legwork, I heard a lot of rumors and picked up plenty of uncorroborated information. What I didn't get was solid evidence to back up my gut feelings. The three suspects took off for Florida before I could question them at any length.

It was then that I had to acquire large amounts of the policeman's friend, patience. When your leads run out, you can't do much more than wait for a break. I was at that point in the Clark case—but the break that came wasn't the kind I had in mind. I was suddenly transferred from the Northamption HQ to the Pittsfield barracks.

Corporal Bob Gustavis caught the responsibility for the Clark case. I felt good about that because I knew he wasn't the type who'd pigeonhole an investigation just because it hadn't been his in the first place. I gave Gustavis everything I had on the case, both officially and off the record. He promised to chase down anything new that developed, and when I left I felt the case was in good hands.

Once in a great while, when our paths would cross in the line of duty, Corporal Gustavis would give me an update on the Clark case. Having interviewed Bob Clark several times, Gustavis too had come to have a soft spot for the old-timer. The corporal had similar suspicions about the trio from the next town that I'd had and alerted his network of informants. Eventually, he came up with a tip from someone close to the suspects, that before they fled for Florida they'd stumbled across approximately two thousand dollars.

The two thousand figure matched what Walter Dzenis and I had calculated would fit in small bills in a cracker box. It looked like we had our boys—if they ever felt the heat was off enough for them to return from Florida. It would have to be under their own steam. The Commonwealth wasn't going to request extradition. Not on the basis of informants' tips and troopers' hunches.

Much to our initial elation, the suspects returned a year later. They were promptly arrested. By this time Gustavis had gathered additional, though unconfirmed, reports reinforcing our opinion of the guilt of two of these suspects. What was needed to tie everything together was positive identification by Bob Clark.

It never happened. Bob felt pretty sure that the two we'd apprehended were his assailants, but his Yankee conscience wouldn't allow him to accuse them as long as he had the least shred of doubt.

"Ain't afraid of those hoods," he said. "They're prob'ly guilty as hell of *something*. But I'd never sleep nights if I was wrong. Besides, the light wasn't so good that day..."

So the pair escaped going to jail. They also escaped my plan for revenge.

When it became obvious that we weren't going to get a conviction in court, I wanted to commit the two to a lifetime of frustration. I knew it would drive greedy weasels like them totally wacko if I casually let it slip that they'd been within touching distance of a hundred thousand preinflation dollars in untraceable cash.

Two thoughts stopped me from inflicting that perfect revenge. One was my belief in our system, however imperfect. I wasn't happy that they got off. But if our system of laws set them free, it wasn't up to me to play vigilante; it was up to me to help build a better case against them next time.

The other thought that stopped me was a fear that they'd try again if they knew Bob Clark still wasn't using banks.

Postscript

About a year later, Corporal Gustavis sent word that he'd finally built a better case and put the two suspects from the Clark case behind bars for a long term. We'd both been so convinced of their guilt that he'd kept them on short rein and eventually nabbed them on another break-in.

Bob Gustavis and I were out of touch for perhaps two years after that before meeting on another investigation. When we'd had a chance to catch up, Bob's first question was if I remembered old man Clark.

"Could I ever forget? Those two still in jail?"

Gustavis nodded. "Then you must also remember Bob Clark's aversion to banks," he said. "Seems he had the same kind of aversion to taxes. Never paid any. The IRS grabbed every cent he had in the bank. Then they took all those little boxes he'd squirreled away in the house. Far as I know, they got it all. Every cent."

I felt sorry for Bob Clark for a long time after that until it occurred to me that money didn't mean anything to him. Perhaps his attitude toward the worth of money is what drew me to old Bob. To others money meant power or what it could buy, including opinion.

To Bob Clark, money had value only insofar as it replenished the supply of tires in his barn. Beyond that, it meant nothing, had no value. After Bob's tires were paid for, money was just something to fill up his cracker boxes.

7. Academy II

The more things change...

Time: Midcareer
Location: Framingham
Duty: Shaping up the troops

From my comfortable vantage in the bedroom of a private suite of the new billets, I watched the arrival of fresh meat, the newest entering class at the Massachusetts State Police Academy. Twenty years had passed since my own first, nerve-wracking days as a recruit. There had been a lot of changes during those years, but the biggest change for me was spelled out on the name plaque on the door of the suite: *Staff Sergeant David Moran/Assistant Commandant.*

Watching the drill instructor prowling before the forming ranks made me think of my own first day, when I stood at rigid attention in front of the old wooden administration building, quivering before Corporal Dzikiewicz as he read off the names of the new recruits. In the intervening twenty years, the WWII quonset huts had given way to a modern three-story structure ample enough to contain a gymnasium, a swimming pool and an indoor firing range. The new recruits would no longer have to stand waiting in long lines outside the mess hall. They now waited for permission to enter, inside, braced against the wall of a long, highly polished corridor. The procedure was the same, but they weren't exposed to the elements as I had been.

The monstrous, open squad bays lined with rows of metal bunks and lockers diabolically designed to abolish privacy were no more.

Instead there were separate sleeping quarters intended for oc-cupancy by only two recruits per unit. The single cavernous classroom jammed with desks was replaced by an air-conditioned, state-of-the-art lecture hall equipped with the latest in audio-visual equipment. Instructors were quartered in their own suites on each floor.

Watching from the large bedroom window of my suite, I could see the same east parking lot where I'd arrived twenty years earlier. Though the physical surroundings had radically changed, the human element seemed to behave about the same. The new ar-rivals, natty in suits and ties, tended to cluster in small groups. Everyone hovered near his luggage as if there were academy trolls assigned to steal it. It seemed so similar. It could have been my class out there in the parking lot. I smiled, imagining they were hashing over the same fears. Like generations of recruits before them, every one of them was hoping to get a little advance poop on the academy training.

My smile broadened. No matter how many people the newcomers had consulted in advance, no matter how truthful those consultants had been, the spirit-crushing reality of the academy's military discipline and intensive physical training far overshadowed any foreknowledge. Regardless of how fantasy-laden a recruit's information about the academy might be, he had to learn for himself, and the learning was always worse than the fantasy.

At precisely 0900 hours, four spit and polish drill instructors ap-peared in front of the recent civilians. With swagger sticks and loud command voices, the instructors began forming them into separate squads. They made four ranks according to height and told them to face left. Once satisfied they could move without fall-ing over, the DIs marched them around the rear of the building toward the lecture hall. At that point they'd be out of my field of vision, but I knew exactly what procedures would be followed. Halting in front of the lecture hall they would be told to leave their luggage out on the pavement of the company street and file in to be seated at desks piled high with all the required reading matter for their courses. Then they'd be told to wait in silence.

It was time for me to meet them officially. I turned from the window to check my spotless uniform in the full-length mirror on the back of the door, standard equipment in academy rooms. Snatching my campaign hat and swagger stick from the spring-taut blanket on the bunk, I started for the commandant's office.

Striding along the gleaming corridor toward the stairwell, I automatically made a visual check of every room I passed. The troop billets were comfortable, but sufficiently devoid of civilian amenities to be considered Spartan. Each room had two single-frame bunks with pillow, linen and blankets precisely folded at the foot of each. There was a large wall locker assigned to each recruit as well as a small desk, lamp and chair. The arrangement of the furniture was prescribed beforehand and not to be tampered with. The drill instructors periodically checked each piece of furniture, going so far as to measure its distance from the wall. It was imperative that troopers learn to pay attention to detail. The regimen of military discipline and insistence on precision practiced at the academy were the best method of teaching respect for the importance of detail and ingraining it as a habit. The habit was known to save lives.

I started down the stairs. There were sixty double rooms on the two floors, room enough for one hundred and twenty recruits. This class would begin with an even hundred recruits, but experience had proven that the number would begin to diminish even by the end of the first day.

I entered the commandant's office off the main corridor of the first floor. The boss trooper at the academy was Captain Robert E. Dunn, the same Dunn, Robert E., who'd shagged his tail around the academy track when he and I were recruits together. His desk was flanked by the state and national flags, or colors, as we called them in this quasi-military setting. Captain Dunn looked up from a never-ending pile of paperwork as I entered smartly.

"Captain, the new class is ready for you in the lecture hall."

"Well, Sergeant," Dunn said as he stood up, a hint of a smile playing across his lips. "I think we're ready for them, too." Together we marched to the lecture hall.

Corporal Thompson, the director of recruit training, was stationed near the front door, primed for our arrival. As we entered he barked at the assembly: "On your feet, people!"

At the sound of Thompson's scream, the already-apprehensive recruits bolted upright, trying to outdo each other in obedience to the corporal's command. In their panic, they banged their knees and elbows into the desks, spilling piles of books and papers. Trying to recover from their confusion they made things worse. There was pandemonium.

Captain Dunn waited near the door while I strode through the confusion to the raised podium. I jumped up and stood surveying the roomful of anxious, awkward recruits. It seemed impossible that in twenty short weeks these men would acquire the poise and bearing of service academy cadets.

Corporal Thompson yelled, "Seats!"

I gripped the lectern, watching the bewildered recruits as they struggled to get back down into their desks without knocking anything over. When the room settled, I introduced myself and Corporal Thompson. Then I identified the instructors by name: Troopers Ardita, McNulty, Murphy and Redfern. The instructors, standing at parade rest along the rear wall of the lecture hall, each snapped to attention and took one step forward as I went through the staff roster: Donovan, DeFava, Jones, Walsh, McLean. The recruits craned their necks to see the academy's legendary drill instructors snap to as their names were called. I carefully observed protocol, introducing the instructors in order of seniority.

"Now I'd like to introduce the Commandant of the Academy." I stepped down from the podium as Captain Dunn moved for the stage. The recruits repeated the whole unwieldy business of rising and sitting. Captain Dunn smiled indulgently, waiting. He knew how nerve-wracking the first few hours on academy turf could be.

"I welcome each of you to the Massachusetts State Police Academy. You are fortunate to have been selected for training in one of the finest police organizations in this country. You will be training in the finest police academy in the United States, staffed by the best instructors. It's our job to train you so that you measure up to the standards of the State Police and that you meet our expectations of excellence," the Captain began. I watched the intent expressions on the recruits' faces as Dunn continued.

"Created in 1865, we are the oldest state police in the United States—and, I think, the best. We didn't win our superb reputation as a training facility by being a country club. The training is strenuous and difficult. But it has a valid purpose. As a state trooper you must at all times be confident, resourceful and self-reliant on the job. You will have to perform many tasks and make many decisions on your own.

You may be assigned to a lonely rural area with the nearest barracks many miles and many minutes away. Most often you'll be alone with no back-up to call upon. Most emergencies you'll be required to handle yourself. You'd better be good.

"The continuation of our fine reputation depends on the product we turn out. We'll graduate only the best," Dunn said. I knew the Captain was wrapping up his welcome, and I waited for the famous turnpike admonition that my own recruit class had heard, and countless others would hear. Captain Dunn didn't disappoint.

"If you are not ready to give this academy 100 percent effort, I would suggest you leave now," he said. "Route 9, which is in front of this complex, runs east and west, the width of this Commonwealth. Either direction should take you back close to where you came from. To those of you here for the duration, good luck."

I gave the order signaling the end of the welcome.

"Corporal Thompson, take charge of the class."

Commandant Dunn and I marched out past the lined-up instructors into the company street, weaving our way through the silent formation of luggage.

8. The Lottery

That's show biz...

Time: Anytime
Location: Western Massachusetts
Duty: Learning the ropes

Like people in show business, troopers often succeed more because of luck than talent or training. As many major crimes are solved by someone being in the right place at the right time as they are by astute detective work—though the luckiest troopers seem to be the ones who work the hardest.

Good luck is greatly appreciated in police work because the frustration level is so high. Time after time officers will bust their humps to bring a criminal to justice only to see him slip through the cracks of the legal system, either because of some technicality or the machinations of some crafty lawyer. But once in a while Lady Luck will smile, and one of the good guys will hit the lottery.

One of those times began on a routine night tour of duty at the Pittsfield barracks. I was having coffee with Trooper Todd Bell and Staff Sergeant Gloria Kennedy when the shift commander, Sergeant Perch, stuck his head in the guardroom.

"North Adams Police just called," Perch began, his worried expression alerting us to the gravity of his message. "Two guys tied up and robbed a woman in her home, in Clarksburg. S'posed to be headed this way in a silver VW bug. Believed armed."

Trooper Bell rose from the table. Slipping into his winter reefer coat, he strapped on his gun.

"A silver Volkswagen, huh? Shouldn't be too hard to spot in this neck of the woods. Guess I'll have to be the one," he announced nonchalantly. "I'll just go out and grab them."

The rest of us laughed at Bell's braggadocio, not because he wasn't a capable cop—he was as capable as any one of us—but because he meant to be funny by the sheer preposterousness of his statement. To begin with, Clarksburg lay thirty miles north of Pittsfield barracks. None of us had any idea how much of a head start the alleged criminals had, or even what direction they were headed in. They could be headed into Vermont or New York state, down to Connecticut or in a different direction inside Massachusetts. The chances of Bell going out and actually being in the right place to apprehend these guys were about the same as Mickey Rooney faking out Larry Bird one-on-one on the Celtics' home court. In truth, it was simply Bell's way of announcing coffee break was over and he was going back on patrol.

Shortly after Bell had left the station, Gloria Kennedy departed for her office in Northampton. She barely had her cruiser rolling when trooper Todd Bell's voice came squawking over the radio.

"Cruiser 116 to L-4. I'm stopping a silver VW, at Coltsville," he said, naming a well-known nearby junction.

I flipped, hearing his call on the barracks radio. Here was Bell, gone less than five minutes, and he actually *was* stopping the suspects. Incredible!

Remembering the warning from North Adams PD—"suspects believed to be armed"—I jumped up to go help Bell. Lucky bastard. I couldn't believe anybody could be so dumb lucky, but at the same time I was nervous about him stopping armed suspects by himself.

Speed is of the utmost when a fellow trooper is even potentially in trouble. I wanted to be there immediately. I double-timed out of the barracks. Jumping into my cruiser I roared down Dalton avenue. The Coltsville intersection was only a mile away. Approaching the intersection I wondered which branch of the junction Bell was on.

"What's your location, Todd?" I shouted into my radio mike, instinctively turning north on Route 8, toward North Adams. Unseen by me on a different branch of the four-way, Sergeant Kennedy watched me fly by.

"You're heading the wrong way, Dave," she radioed, calling me back to where she was with Bell and the suspects. So much for instinct. I only cut off about six cars as I executed a wheel-screeching U-turn in the middle of the busy intersection. For a minute it looked like a silent movie chase scene, only with me causing all the confusion. I hoped the desk jockeys back at the barracks didn't hear the radio jive about me heading the wrong way. I finally joined Sergeant Kennedy and Trooper Bell.

Already rolling when Bell had called in, Gloria Kennedy was at Bell's side almost immediately. She had blocked off the road with her cruiser and Todd Bell had both the suspects spread-eagled beside their car.

"Take a peek inside, Dave." Smiling, Todd Bell gestured to the floor of the VW bug. There was a note of restrained triumph in his voice.

A canvas money bag with a North Adams bank logo lay on the car floor. Protruding from under the driver's seat was the unmistakable knurled butt of a .38 caliber pistol. Halleluiah!

It's difficult to describe a policeman's elation at a time like this. Even in these days of often-exaggerated regard for the perpetrator's rights, that arrest would be considered a cop's dream. We had the suspects, evidence, a weapon and probable cause, the whole *megillah*. And everything was being done by the book. We weren't going to lose this one to some bleeding-heart lawyer.

Using Todd Bell's handcuffs as well as my own, I secured the suspects, then helped Bell finish a weapons search. We had found the gun on the floor, but they may have also carried knives or another gun. Satisfied the situation was secure, Sergeant Kennedy continued on to Northampton. Bell and I separated the men, each of us returning to Pittsfield barracks with a prisoner.

Despite the evidence, when questioned, neither man would admit much more than his name and address—Eugene X and Mark Y, both from Springfield, Massachusetts. Given the fairly standard MO of home robberies, we were at first puzzled why the two had traveled all the way from Springfield to pull off the job. That item got cleared up sooner than we expected.

Immediately after the call to Pittsfield barracks that initiated our involvement in the case, Sergeant Perch had pulled Trooper

Jim Leonard off his assigned patrol in Savoy. Perch then dispatched Trooper Leonard to the North Adams regional hospital to interview the victim, Mrs. Wilson. Trooper Leonard wasn't allowed an extensive interview with the victim because she suffered from a heart condition that was further aggravated by her rough treatment at the hands of the thieves. Her physician was concerned that she could have another heart attack at any time. She was especially vulnerable to stress.

During the brief time he was allowed to interview the victim, Leonard managed to learn that Mrs. Wilson had easily recognized one of the perpetrators. She was certain because he'd been an employee in her husband's lumber business. Our prisoner, Eugene, was a perfect match for her physical description of the man—and happened to have the same name as well.

Leonard also learned the crooks had stolen a unique coin collection from the Wilsons. If we could find such an easily identifiable item like that, our job of tying these lads to the crime would be a lot easier.

Trooper Leonard reported that Mrs. Wilson seemed severely traumatized by the incident. He said her fear was particularly extreme as she could not shake the terror of her ordeal. She tearfully related that the one named Mark had insisted at several points during the holdup that she be murdered so that she could not identify them later. He let her know by gesture and expression that it would be his pleasure.

Officer Leonard knew as well as anyone what was needed to solidify Mrs. Wilson's statement, and our case. We needed her to positively identify the suspects from among a group. But Jim Leonard had to return with his reluctant opinion that her doctor was right. It was impossible in her present physical condition to come in for a line-up. At that time we didn't know that it would never be possible. But of course we weren't volunteering or sharing that information with our prisoners. When we decided we'd gotten all we were going to get from Mark and Eugene, we let them sit in their cells for a while and sweat out what we might know.

Due to the incomplete questioning of the victim, Mrs. Wilson, it was impossible for us to know at this point in the case how thoroughly she'd been terrorized by the assailants. But we soon found out she was totally convinced they meant to kill her. The situation was especially galling since her husband had treated the former employee, Eugene, very well.

Mrs. Wilson was an invalid who posed no physical threat to her attackers. It would have made sense for them simply to take her money and other valuables and scram, standard behavior for housebreak artists. But Mrs. Wilson was strapped to a chair and repeatedly subjected to escalating verbal threats. As though torture was more important than the loot, they spent precious time going into lurid and gory detail about what they'd do to her if she squealed on them. They also kept poking their knife at her eyes and making wild, slashing motions across the front of her face. Mrs. Wilson later gave a convincing deposition stating that at several separate points in her captivity she was positive they were about to kill her. They doubled their cruelty by screaming wild threats that brought her to the brink of despair, backing off till she calmed, then starting again. Added to all that, she was afraid for her husband's life too, as they kept warning her they'd kill him as well if he happened home before they left.

So our suspects had good reason to sweat it out in their cells. In the meantime we found new reason for jubilation. Hidden under the seat of the crime car was the Wilson's stolen coin collection. Unique, it was evidence that was practically incontrovertible. To back up his verbal report, Wilson had, at a prior date, inventoried and described his coin collection so thoroughly and in such detail that they could only have come from there, nowhere else.

All we needed was his wife's eyewitness testimony to back up our stack of circumstantial evidence, and we could put these guys away forever. We were feeling super. Within two hours from the time I'd raced from the barracks to help out Todd Bell, we'd apprehended the suspects and, it seemed, collected all the evidence we needed to convict our prisoners. Any time things go that smoothly in the war against the bad guys, you feel like you've hit the million-dollar lottery. And that's about how often there are no hitches.

About the time our elbows were giving out from patting ourselves on the back, I was summoned to the cell area. Our duty jailer informed me that, the suspect who had once worked in Wilson's lumber business, Eugene wanted to see me. Being on a roll, I felt it had to be good news. I figured he'd had time to consider all the evidence against him and he wanted to plea bargain, make a deal. Or else remorse for his despicable actions had set in and he wanted to repent. I went back to the cellblock half expecting a confession. Our superiors would probably write up a letter of commendation for both Bell and me on this one. Sure would look good in my file, I thought.

Never happened.

Eugene was waiting for me in his cell, a nervous, animal look on his face, as if he expected to be shot any minute for his despicable crime. I have to admit I never found a little healthy fear any harm when questioning suspects.

Eugene had a gravelly voice, but his tone was timid as he asked, "How is she?"

"Who?"

"Boss's wife, Mrs. Wilson. Only tryin' to scare her a little bit."

I sensed that Eugene wanted to talk about the incident, either for catharsis or to explain himself as the nicer one of the pair. If his eyes were a tip-off to his mental condition, then maybe I could get a confession out of him, or at least get him to rat on his partner. There was a desperate look in his eye that I felt expressed an awareness that this time he'd gone too far, was in over his head. Or he could have been feeling sorry.

"She's fine," I lied, "No thanks to you and your partner. Want to tell me about it?"

That was the moment when I thought it'd go our way. Eugene looked ready to cave, but. . .

His partner, Mark, was housed in a contiguous cell; he could see even if he couldn't hear. I don't know if it was just poor timing or if he sensed Eugene was up to something, but that was the moment Mark chose to come to the bars separating the men. When he stood up I knew the chances of getting anything out of Eugene had just gone a'glimmering. Mark made me a prophet by glaring threateningly at his partner, just in case.

"No," Eugene said to my inquiry, reading the body language from the next cell. He shook his head and dropped to his bunk. "I don't want to talk."

Somebody seeking to glorify punks, or make them out to be some sort of mythic folk heroes, someone who purports all criminals are misunderstood minorities out for economic parity, might stylize his silence as *omerta* or code of honor. Bullshit. The punk was afraid his partner would waste him if he squealed.

And that was that.

A month later we were ready to go before a grand jury in Berkshire County. We were; our star witness wasn't. By then, we'd learned what animals the two suspects had been in their treatment of Mrs. Wilson. The more we found out, the more eager we were to see them behind bars, to see justice done. The word sleazeball was invented for these two. Our frustration level was reaching the spillover point because the more eager we became to put this vermin away, the more we were made aware that it was probably an impossibility.

Regardless of the quality of the physical evidence—the loot, the coin collection traceable to Mr. Wilson, the gun—it just wasn't enough. We knew that even a lawyer fresh from the bar exam could get this case thrown out of court without the testimony of the eyewitness. Everything was circumstantial—simply our word against theirs unless Mrs. Wilson appeared against them in court. It was all but certain she'd never testify. We had a big problem.

Beyond our involvement, testifying about the arrest procedure and evidence acquired, Todd Bell and I were supposed to be emotionally and physically detached from this case. But of course we weren't. We had turned the case over to the prosecuting arm of the law, but we were still emotionally involved, hoping to see justice done on our bust.

Of course we try to be objective and, for the most part, we are able to separate personal prejudice from duty objectives. I'd imagine the majority of police do that better than most people. But to pretend a policeman remains totally objective on every case strains belief. Naturally you follow a case you made a bust on more closely than the ones you know nothing about. If an officer told me he didn't, I'd want to check his locker to see what he's numbing out on.

Technically though, once the arrest was made the problem was no longer ours. It had become the baby of Assistant District Attorney Bill Flynn. Flynn was one of the good guys; he really cared about justice and he really cared about people. Sitting in his office listening to him complain about the official reports he'd received from the cardiologists and psychiatrists attending Mrs. Wilson, it was easy to see that Flynn was as frustrated as we were.

"The heart doctor says she'll have a stress heart attack if we make her testify, and her shrink almost guarantees that the trauma of being face to face with those two in court would push her over the edge forever," Bill said gruffly. But the sad cast to his eyes belied the gruffness. You knew he could never pull underhanded lawyer's tricks or force someone to testify if it would harm her. He shook his head in resignation. "I'd like to nail those two—but without Mrs. Wilson, it'll never happen."

Flynn was right. Todd and I could only testify to what we actually saw. That meant we could probably help find them guilty of possession of stolen money and illegal possession of a firearm, but that was it. The only person who could actually testify to either the actual robbery or the threat of murder was the victim, Mrs. Wilson. It was a case where the inhumanity of the criminals worked in their favor. The potential witness had been so frightened, the terror of the ordeal had left her a quivering, fearful shell.

Todd asked, "Can we at least get her in here for the grand jury?"

The D.A.'s office couldn't even order the culprits brought to trial without first having an indictment handed down by the grand jury stating there was enough evidence of a crime to justify tax-payers' money being spent in court.

Flynn shrugged. "Her doctors might go for that. They know that a grand jury appearance isn't like a trial. The witness is not in the courtroom with the accused." He shook his head again. "Don't know what good that'll do, if she still won't testify later at the trial."

We put our heads together and came up with a sort of plan. Unsure of what action to take, yet not wanting to let go entirely, we decided that we'd just take things a step at a time and see what developed.

The D.A. prevailed, at least temporarily. After we assured the doctors and family that she wouldn't be testifying in sight of the suspects, Mrs. Wilson appeared before a grand jury. The day of the hearing, Mrs. Wilson was wheeled into the grand jury room on a gurney. Her two doctors stood beside her while the assistant district attorney speedily took her testimony and excused her. Trooper Bell and I saw her in the hallway afterwards. Pale and shaking, fear etched in her face, she pulled her blanket tightly around herself as if that would protect her from the wicked world. She was a frail reed. What griped us the most was knowing how she's been made that way and what little chance we had of being able to do anything about it.

Sharing a smoke while waiting for the grand jury's decision, her husband told us that since the robbery, Mrs. Wilson could not be left home alone. In order for him to go to work he had to hire someone to sit with her until his return.

"Don't know if she'll ever be able to shake those phantoms out of her head," Wilson said. "Literally jumps at shadows, poor thing."

Todd and I exchanged secret looks of surrender. No matter what the grand jury decided, we knew Mrs. Wilson could never survive a trial. Our thoughts were confirmed when D.A. Bill Flynn came out of the grand jury room. At the door, he was accosted by the Wilson woman's angry cardiologist. The doctor vehemently reiterated his opinion of his patient's inability to withstand a trial.

"Look at her from just this hearing," he said.

Todd and I pulled the harried attorney around the corner.

"We got the indictments we wanted. Armed robbery and threat to murder," Flynn said. "But what good they'll do us, I don't know. We can never go to trial."

Annoyed with our bad luck, dejected that Mark and Eugene would either walk free or receive negligible sentences for the minor possession offenses, we walked across the street to drown our sorrows in beer.

From there on, the script read out about as expected. Mark and Eugene were held at the house of correction while awaiting trial. They hired the best attorney money could buy. It seemed only a matter of time before they'd be back out on the streets terrorizing innocent people. Despair was the order of the day for Flynn, Todd Bell and me.

Suffice it to say we weren't in the highest of spirits for the pretrial conference, where the lawyers do some of their preliminary work, setting the ground rules for the trial to come, and where plea bargaining often takes place. At the conference we were treated to a meeting with Harvey Silver, the high-powered lawyer hired by Eugene and Mark. Silver arrived at the Monday morning conference sartorially resplendent in the flashiest, most expensive threads ever seen in Berkshire County. Supremely self-assured and slightly abrasive, Silver blasted away, accusing our side of prejudice and disposing of our testimony as if it were worthless.

The lawyer had a method of questioning that seemed to cast doubt on our testimony, no matter how we answered. Even if you've been a subject of this tactic before, it can still be a difficult time. To cops who pride themselves on their honesty, it's especially gruelling, mentally and emotionally, to be made to look like they would lie or alter testimony in order to railroad a particular subject, even when they know it's a ploy. Some lawyers will do anything to get their clients off—even if it means making the policeman look like a vindictive liar, a habitual drunk or a simpleton.

That day Bell and I felt like strangling Silver and breaking him into little pieces. During the pretrial conference he made it sound as if Bell and I were the guilty parties who had grossly violated his innocent clients' rights by slowing them down at the Coltsville junction. As much as we wanted to throttle Silver we managed to maintain an outward appearance of professional stoicism. After a while on the job you realize that the behavior of most attorneys is not a personal attack but simply one of the tools they use in their attempt to spring clients loose.

I couldn't see why we were wasting our time anyway. Our witness wouldn't testify, and we had no major case without her testimony. So it was only a matter of the type of sentence a judge would hand down for the relatively minor possession counts. It seemed as though Silver was stretching things out rather needlessly. He had to know that we were without a case, that our witness couldn't testify.

He finally stopped haranguing Bell and me. He pulled his chair up to the conference table before dropping his bomb.

"My clients wouldn't be opposed to a guilty plea," he said, rubbing his eyes with the heels of his palms, "if the Commonwealth weren't thinking of pressing for too long a sentence."

What? We couldn't be hearing right—the defense lawyer copping a plea when we didn't have a case? Impossible to be so lucky. Bell and I didn't dare say anything or even look at each other for fear we'd blow it. We hardly dared breathe. Silver must have flipped his wig. He could walk them both right out of there.

Bill Flynn somehow kept his cool. He remained silent, a thoughtful expression on his face, as if he was considering the defense attorney's offer. Flynn had to be every bit as astonished as Bell and I. He deserved an Oscar.

"Gee, Harvey, I don't know. I was really looking forward to trying this case," Flynn said, straightfaced. "Should be open and shut, the evidence we got . . ."

"Nothing's ever that simple, Bill," Attorney Silver said, looking pained.

"Do kinda hate to waste the taxpayers' money needlessly," Flynn said. Flynn turned his back to Silver so that he couldn't see the wink and smile he snuck at Trooper Bell and me.

"I suppose if your boys want to plead guilty, we could go along with it to spare the taxpayer."

I was afraid that Flynn was laying it on too thick or that something would happen and I'd wake up to see that the plea-copping was only a dream. I watched, trancelike, as Flynn jutted out his jaw and leaned menacingly across the table to Silver. I thought he was going too far.

"Mark gets fifteen to twenty—Eugene ten to fifteen," Flynn said. I knew he'd blown it.

Silver scoffed. "C'mon, Bill."

"That's my recommendation to the judge."

"We can't accept that. Ease up a little," Silver protested. "It's way too high; they'd be old men."

"Should have thought of that before they terrorized that poor woman." Flynn remained adamant. I was sure he'd tipped his hand by playing too tough. A glance at Bell's face told me he thought the same way. Should've been happy with the guilty plea and taken what we could get.

Eternity seemed to come and go while Harvey Silver contemplated the district attorney's offer. This was hardball. The two lawyers stared long at each other. It was Silver's shoulders that sagged. "Okay, we'll take the deal."

Minutes later, lawyer Silver departed for the house of correction to explain the Commonwealth's new extended vacation plan to his clients. Gentlemen that we were, and afraid of a last-minute change of mind, we waited until Harvey Silver's footsteps no longer echoed down the marble-floored hallway. Finally sure that he was out of earshot, Todd Bell leaped to his feet screaming.

"We won—we won! We won the lottery!"

9. The Body

I could have sworn she was dead...

Time: Autumn
Location: Enfield cemetery
Duty: Breast examination

Anyone who has ever spent time swapping stories with policemen soon realizes that he hears more humorous anecdotes than war stories or tales of derring-do. Like the combat veteran whose memory favors the good times he spent partying with his buddies rather than the horrors of war, the policeman tends to tell stories that concentrate on the amusing things that happen in his daily routine.

Police humor is often of the gallows variety, but making light of the tragedy you encounter every day seems to make the job bearable and keep you hanging in there. If everything that happened was taken too seriously, without the relief of humor, the burden of the job would soon pave the road to a mental institution. Doctors, nurses, firemen, ambulance drivers, clergymen—all who serve or see the public in their unwashed state share a sense of humor that to a civilian borders on callousness. Their daily exposure to the vagaries of the human condition and the way people sometimes mistreat each other gives them a perspective that isn't shared by all of polite society.

A policeman's sense of tragedy and comedy is shaped less by what's on the tube than what's really happening on the streets. He deals with life. People in police work and related fields are, above all, realists. What they see and experience is what really is, not someone else's romanticized version of what should be. So, twisted though it may often seem, their sense of humor is the required antidote to terminal cynicism.

Much police humor arises from routine foul-ups, minor problems that bear little resemblance to the high-paced action of television. Hollywood rarely shows day-to-day police work as it truly is. Focusing on high-impact drama, television shows and movies never present a picture of the petty organizational jealousy that can exist between departments with overlapping or concurrent jurisdictions; nor do they show simple, routine errors or long, quiet nights.

True episodes like that would get most cop shows canceled before October. Of course, the intense pitch of drama and excitement required for "Hill Street Blues" is sustained for a mere sixty minutes, minus commercial messages. Let television cops try it for 44 to 104 hours a week some time.

Despite the impression given by television, real police officers don't shoot innocent bystanders every day; nor do they perpetually prosecute and jail the wrong persons. Not every department is riddled by addictions to alcohol, drugs or gambling. Neither are all police compromised by bribery, graft or sex. I don't pretend to say those things don't happen or that they don't all exist. Divorce is rampant among police personnel, and the rate of alcohol and drug abuse is just as high, if not higher, than it is among the general population.

But while all of these highly dramatic things have been known to happen somewhere sometime, most screw-ups are far more mundane, like taking someone into protective custody for public intoxication when in fact he is suffering from temporary hypoglycemia. Granted, that's not *Beverly Hills Cop.*

In my experience your routine police foul-up is an argument, a jurisdictional dispute involving an officer from a different department or precinct over responsibility for the paperwork on a car accident. Not exactly high drama. Another typical screw-up often occurs when there's disagreement over who is in charge in the territory involved. Sometimes it can seem like kids in a sandbox, as I found out when I crossed paths with some of my rural counterparts.

Excluding New Hampshire, state police in New England have jurisdictional problems that exist nowhere else in the United

States. Troopers in the remaining five states have what is termed Comprehensive Law Enforcement Authority. They are legally authorized to enter, patrol and function in any city or town within their state's boundaries. Furthermore, they can make an arrest or otherwise function as a police entity in those municipalities—even in towns that already have their own established police forces.

With such a system, imagine the potential for jurisdictional friction that exists between the various state and county and municipal departments in New England, especially compared to the simplicity of the Midwest or West, where highway patrols are restricted to state highways by legislative mandate and statute.

Except for some jail personnel, county police and sheriff patrols don't exist in Massachusetts. The duties performed by county or sheriff forces in other parts of the country are done by state troopers. The troopers are not geographically limited, a situation that can create serious disputes among departments if one, or both, are jealously guarding their turf. Fortunately, state troopers follow an unwritten gentlemen's agreement: "We try not to go where we're not wanted."

The state force consciously avoids potentially embarrassing situations by keeping their patrols out of those cities and towns that have established police forces except in cases of invitation or public emergency. Even though troopers have the legal authority to intervene, this policy has proven a wise and workable one over the years.

In the more sparsely populated western part of the state, where the local police departments are small or even nonexistent, locals and state troopers have a mutually beneficial working relationship. The area trooper and the locals usually know each other on a first-name basis and often form lasting friendships that extend beyond the job. Of course there are also some individuals for whom the chemistry just isn't right, who become involved in incidents that strain interdepartmental amity. One such incident that I experienced, though a good example of police humor, was also indicative of the conflicts troopers can have with other police forces.

It had been a very quiet tour. I was out in the boonies in western Massachusetts, parked atop Windsor mountain. Windsor sits across from Mount Greylock, the highest point in Massachusetts. High up in the Berkshire mountain range, the town of Savoy was at the eastern limit of my patrol out of Pittsfield barracks.

Far from the transmitter at Northampton, I had the volume set at maximum in case the barracks tried to contact me. I had forgotten about the transmitter for Pittsfield barracks. The sudden blast of sound almost blew me out of the cruiser.

"Station L4 to cruiser 419!—signal 6."

I leapt for the volume knob to tone it down. The sound was deafening. L4 was Pittsfield barracks' call sign. I was sitting practically on top of Pittsfield's powerful transmitter, located on Mt. Greylock, just over my shoulder at 3,450 feet above sea level.

I was cruiser 419. Signal 6 was a request for my location. I waited a few seconds for the roaring in my ears to stop.

"419. Cheshire Road, Windsor," I answered, wondering what was so urgent that Pittsfield was trying to raise me, since I was on extra patrol. I also wondered if I'd ever hear again.

"You know the Larchmont cemetery in Enfield, 419?

"Affirmative, L4," I answered, not liking the sound of this already.

"The Enfield force is tied up. Proceed forthwith to cemetery. Possible suicide, or suicide attempt."

That's all they had. I revved up and headed down the mountain roads toward Route 8 for the cemetery in Enfield.

It wasn't at all unusual to get a request for help from one of the smaller towns in our patrol area, but it was extremely rare to get a call from this particular town, Enfield. The Enfield chief was famous for his low regard for state troopers and his high estimation of his own authority in the territory. Any time his force and ours had met in Pittsfield District Court, relations were strained. So I was puzzled over the call, but I raced toward the suicide attempt. I figured there must be a real crime wave going on in little Enfield if both their duty cruisers and the chief were tied up at the same time.

At the time I didn't know that the Enfield dispatcher called the state troopers for help because he had a definite crisis on his hands and couldn't raise either of the town's two cruisers over the air. He'd checked the station's transmitter, which wasn't at fault. His men just weren't answering. It must have been a tough decision for the guy because he knew that the chief would want his head for calling in outsiders.

Despite a fairly widespread spirit of cooperation between state and local departments, some local, long-standing resentment toward the state troopers still existed because of their superior training and equipment and their healthier budgets. Then, too, on our side there was always a certain number of trooper snobs who considered the locals as hopelessly inept yokels who wouldn't know a serious crime if they tripped over it. As in anything else, there was some truth on both sides.

True or not, in the chief's mind calling us would be tantamount to admitting he couldn't handle things within his jurisdiction and had to come running for help. For certain law enforcement types, admitting the need for help is about as appealing as it is to the stereotypical, macho military mindset. Help translates to interference. We didn't look at it that way, but someone jealous or insecure enough might. Especially someone like the Enfield chief who wasted no love on the state force to begin with.

The reason for the urgency, I later found out, was that the dispatcher had received a call from a woman hysterically shouting about a suicide. When the deskman calmed her down enough to understand her, he learned that the caller's grieving sister, despondent over her husband's recent death, was threatening suicide. According to the caller, her sister had said:

"I'm going to do it over his grave, then I'll always be right next to him. Forever!"

After several frantic minutes of trying to raise the police chief or the cruisers, the dispatcher had reluctantly radioed the staties at Pittsfield. At the time, I wasn't privy to that background information.

Turning off Route 8 into the cemetery, I was surprised to see the blue lights of a cruiser already there ahead of me. I pulled up behind the Enfield black-and-white, figuring the dispatcher must've finally raised his men after sending us the SOS. Maybe they hadn't gotten around to cancelling my orders to respond. I felt sorry for the dispatcher, imagining what he'd be in for from his chief, all for trying to do the right thing. I also wondered what the local cops had been doing that they couldn't be reached. Screwing off, if I knew this pair.

They stood about twenty yards away, talking to each other among the headstones. If they'd been sleeping somewhere, you'd think they would have had enough sense for one of them to stay awake to listen to the radio. Getting out of my cruiser, I offered a comradely salutation. I'm a great believer in cooperation.

"Need any help, boys?"

Walking toward them I could now see they were standing over the inert figure of a woman sprawled across a newly filled-in gravesite. It looked like she'd carried out her suicide plans before the cavalry could arrive to stop her.

Neither Enfield cop responded to my greeting. With typical professional courtesy they walked around me and got back in their cruiser, simply ignoring me as I approached the gravesite. I bent down over the woman, figuring I might as well have a look, seeing how I nearly committed suicide myself trying to get there. She was sprawled across the grave on her back. Bending close, I saw the small entrance hole chest-high on her white sweatshirt. Near the body, one on each side, lay two .22 caliber revolvers. I guessed she wanted to be sure.

But as I bent over the woman it struck me that her coloring was unlike any other corpse I'd ever seen, unless she was so newly dead that her cheeks hadn't even begun to fade. Something didn't seem quite right. In the meantime the sight of the two cruisers in their town cemetery was drawing a crowd of Enfield onlookers. Word must have spread quickly, because in the few minutes I'd been there what looked to be about fifty people had gathered around the gravesite, gawking over at the body and, I suppose, comparing actual police procedure with what they'd seen on television.

"Keep back please—we need room," I shouted, using my command voice.

The onlookers kept a respectful distance then, but their presence made me feel I should be doing something, as if they'd misinterpret my thoroughness as just not knowing what to do.

My attention was diverted momentarily by a squawk from the radio in the Enfield cruiser, parked twenty yards away. Glancing back to the prone form, I detected what seemed to be the flicker of an eyelash—from the corpse! Couldn't be, I thought. I stared ... she blinked!

As her eyelids slowly lifted, she focused momentarily on me, squatting over her, then snapped her eyes shut. Jumped-up Jesus, she wasn't dead, she was playing possum! Were my eyes deceiving me? I yanked up her sweatshirt. I saw a hole in her bra that corresponded with the one in her outer shirt. I pushed the brassiere aside. There was a small hole just above the woman's breast. It was obviously from the .22, but she wasn't even bleeding!

I realized the woman must be in shock because she hadn't even flinched when I jerked the bra up. Her eyes were closed again. I covered her immediately. The cover was to treat for shock but, also aware of the crowd, I wanted to shield them from a glimpse of her seminakedness. What the hell was with those Enfield cops—were they asleep? Hadn't they even bothered to take her vital signs? Had they just assumed she was dead? Or maybe they knew she was still alive and went to call medical help.

It looked like we could save her after all, but she had to get to a hospital, fast. I jumped up, running for the radio.

I was intercepted by the local cops on their way back from their cruiser.

"Whatcher hurry, Trooper?"

Excited, I shouted, "Ambulance en route?"

"Ambulance, hell," one cop said, holding up a big rubber raincoat. "This's to cover the body till the medical examiner gets here. She's dead."

"She's not dead," I exploded. "Get an ambulance here—fast"

The expression on my face must have convinced them I wasn't BS'ing. They didn't argue—they moved. I grabbed the first-aid kit out of my cruiser.

After calling the ambulance, the two locals hustled back. They were all professional now, solicitous of my opinion and help, extremely conscious of the presence of the local crowd. They busied themselves needlessly, helping me bandage the victim's wound. Like it really took three of us to patch a hole the size of a pencil eraser. I suppose they felt it was better than standing around with their thumbs in their mouths waiting for the ambulance to come for their "suicide victim."

The ambulance was blessedly fast. Arriving within minutes of the call, they backed in through the crowd, loaded the woman on a gurney and whisked her off to the Berkshire Medical Center.

Now feeling sorry for them, I figured the local guys'd had enough of my needle, so I kept my mouth shut as I packed up the first-aid kit. The wisdom of my pity became evident almost immediately. The Enfield chief's car pulled in just after the ambulance sped out of the cemetery.

Chief John Walker was a large, sixtyish, red-faced man partial to Manhattan cocktails and accustomed to strict obedience from the members of his force. As police chief of a small town, he was sensitive to his image before a gathered crowd. The trick is to appear, at least, to be in charge.

Chief Walker didn't appear too happy to be called away from his preprandial cocktails in the first place, but the additional thrill of seeing me present in my state trooper uniform darkened his complexion a bit more.

"Who called the State Police?" He barked.

The chief's voice rolled over the spectators. Walker never simply spoke, he boomed. I noticed that the two cops who'd just recently been so helpful with the bandages were sort of melting toward the rear of the crowd. No one answered the chief's boom.

"Well, where's this suicide they called me about," he said, playing to the spectators. "Where's the body?"

Annoyed at the chief's theatrics, I decided to play his game, too.

"What body's that, Chief?" I asked smoothly, eyeing the crowd for their reaction. There's a little Polish ham in me, too.

The spectators were in on the joke; they knew the woman wasn't dead—and they knew the chief didn't know. It was a great chance for them to get a little something back at someone with as much sway in their lives as a small town chief had. At the same time they were, like me, working off some of the adrenalin released by the cemetery incident and the subsequent relief that a neighbor hadn't killed herself. They snickered knowingly, hoping the chief would dig himself in a little deeper. By now the Enfield cops had retreated all the way back to their cruiser.

"Godammit, Trooper—you know the body I'm lookin' for!" Red-faced, sputtering, he spun around. He was looking for his own officers and frustrated that he couldn't get me for insubordination because I wasn't one of his cops. "The suicide—where is she?"

"Oh, *that* body. Well, Chief, that *body*," I couldn't resist playing it broadly, "that body's in an ambulance on the way to the emergency room."

The spectators loved it, but I could see murder blossoming in the chief's eyes as he began to catch on. Believing in the wisdom and advantage of timing, I handed glowering Chief Walker the two revolvers and got the hell out of there before he decided to use them.

There was a happy postscript to this cemetery tale. The woman who had tried to kill herself was eventually released from the hospital, fully recovered from the self-inflicted wound. With help, she was reconciled to the loss of her husband. The ego wounds suffered by the two Enfield cops were probably worse than her bullet wound. Although I crossed paths with them many times after the incident, they never thanked me for saving them the embarrassment and ridicule they'd surely have suffered if the medical examiner had lifted the rubber coat and the expected corpse was sticking her tongue out at him, or something equally bizarre. Afterwards I always felt that I detected an impish look in the woman's eye when I caught her looking at him. Despite the obvious fact that she'd shot herself, I suspected that she had only craved some attention, expecting her family at the grave to stop her before things got out of hand. The actual shooting was probably an accident.

Surprisingly, Chief Walker and I became friends. Shortly after I fled the cemetery, the chief learned the truth about how I happened to be on the scene. Chief Walker had initially thought it was a case of the staties interfering in his jurisdiction, but when he learned that I was merely responding to the summons for aid sent out by the chief's own dispatcher, he was at least mollified, though never overtly apologetic. He even admitted that the state aid was necessary because his own men were indeed screwing off. In time he devised an appropriate punishment for them. I believed him and it didn't bother me that I wasn't thanked.

A mutually respectful, rough-and-ready friendship developed between us. The gruff chief and I shared many an off-duty cocktail together on the chief's mountain view porch where I learned a great deal about rural police work from Chief Walker.

Neither of us ever mentioned the body that wasn't dead.

10. Drug Bust

I'll have a Snickers...

Time: 1970s
Location: Massachusetts Turnpike
Duty: Border patrol

A dramatic change has taken place in the nature of crime in America over the last twenty-five years. Traditional theories of crime and punishment have been complicated by a drug explosion —a phenomenon so pervasive and omnipresent that it hits at the very core of American society. Drugs are everywhere.

In the 1950s drug use was limited mostly to pockets of subculture. Beatniks, musicians and urban ghetto-dwellers were the only real users of junk, although a more than negligible percentage of suburban housewives were high on speed, prescribed as diet pills. And bennies, reefer and black beauties had been around for a long time.

In the sixties, marijuana, LSD and heroin became the new drugs of choice, and drug use became, if not socially welcomed, an acceptable mode of expressing dissatisfaction with the system. By the end of the sixties virtually any drug was easily obtainable without prescription, and our nation's college campuses were where it was at. The federal government made serious efforts to enforce the laws against narcotics and educate the students, but to no noticeable effect.

A tide of drugs washed over the country. Most of the drugs were from foreign sources, and most of the distribution was aimed at the young. As the decade marched on, the armed forces sent home thousands of civilians-to-be who'd grown solidly addicted while serving in Vietnam.

The seventies saw some lessening in the use of hallucinogens like THC and LSD, but the new generation climbed aboard the cocaine bandwagon while at the same time rediscovering the old standby, and America's favorite, booze.

In the eighties, even the youngest kids are buying cheap street drugs, chemicals like PCP that may contain anything. Alcohol abuse is still number one in size and severity, but it doesn't have the cachet required by the in-crowd. Coke is in. Cocaine has shattered the social barrier that used to exist between "social" users of drugs and the de´classe´ junkie. So-called recreational drugs have made the drug scene more of a melting pot. Not only can everybody do drugs now, but drug use has almost become chic.

Over the years, as usage increased nationally and permeated every strata of society, the efforts of the authorities to stop its spread increased as well, though always a few paces behind. The authorities concentrated on upgrading criminal statutes at both federal and state levels. Various legislatures attempted to stem the rising tide with mandatory sentences, longer sentences and classification of drugs by type. People who sold or distributed drugs became the target of virtually every law enforcement agency in the country. Many police departments sought special training for their communties in the drug prevention field, while a seemingly endless parade of self-styled experts offered quick and easy permanent solutions to the complex and growing problem. But nothing seemed to work.

The criminal element behind the drug escalation thrived. Just as Prohibition had driven up the price of booze and made it a daring and attractive though relatively mild form of social protest, so too had the new widespread use of street drugs created a new class of criminal who took advantage of their illegality. Because drugs were illegal, the supplier could charge fifty to five hundred times more than the drug was actually worth. Once the customers were dependent on the product, then product scarcity, real or manufactured, became a universally dependable means of driving prices to new all-time highs. Addiction became very costly.

The capitalist in this new entrepreneurial class is your friendly dealer. The small-time neighborhood pusher rarely participates in the sharing of the real wealth because he is generally a user himself who sells to others simply to maintain his own habit. Most well-established habits cost a hundred dollars per day and up to maintain. The expense is why most users, regardless of personal income, eventually end up resorting to burglary and armed robbery or extensive white-collar crime.

With the rise of drug-related crime, police face a relatively new type criminal, the "druggie." Drug-related crimes are particularly menacing for police because the druggie, armed or not, cannot be reasoned with and does not play by the same book as the professional crook. Impulsive unpredictable, panicky and desperate for money for his next fix, the new guy is more dangerous to face than, say, the average bank robber who has spent some time considering the angles of a job and how not to get hurt.

Most junkies don't plan any further than the next fix. Their crimes are precipitated by the demands of the addiction, and they usually don't even think about an escape—if they need a fix badly enough to steal, they probably don't care if they get killed in the process. Getting the fix is what counts.

Rural areas, traditionally considered a safe place to raise a family, have become just as dangerous as any urban housing project. Drug use has transmigrated over all economic, social and ethnic barriers. Drugstores, mom and pop convenience stores and small restaurants and gas stations, especially those that run twenty-four hour operations, are targets for addicts anxious for money to resupply.

When assigned to duty on the western end of the Massachusetts Turnpike in the early seventies I figured I was out of the drug crime area. I spent three years patrolling a twenty-three mile strip running between Westfield, Massachusetts and the New York border near Albany. Because the heavy traffic volume turns south onto Route 84 for New York City before it hits Westfield, traffic here is light, and three years is a long time to patrol back and forth on that steep stretch of highway.

Nights brought mostly trucks lumbering up the eight-mile, steep climb from Westfield to the summit at Blandford. From Blandford the rigs could coast downhill the remaining twenty-three miles to the state line. After three years, I knew every bump and crack in the blacktop from the zero marker at the border, to the thirty-four mile marker across from the Westfield barracks. After some time on a detail like that, finding a car in the breakdown lane was a welcome relief to the monotony.

We were using 440 cubic inch Chrysler cruisers then, and I could cover that thirty-four mile stretch in about fifteen minutes with both eyes closed. I was cruising westbound toward the border late one tour, wishing for some action. When I spotted a VW in the breakdown lane, I decelerated, flipped on the flashers and rolled to a stop behind it, glad for a break in the tedium.

The vehicle was dark and empty, with no signs of emergency. I stepped smartly back to my warm cruiser to call in a stolen vehicle check. At that altitude it doesn't take long at three in the morning to make a trooper wonder why he didn't become a schoolteacher or office worker with regular, indoor hours.

"Cruiser 126 to station M." My radio transmission signal was bounced from Blandford to Boston on microwave relay dishes. The froggy voice of the dispatcher told me I had dragged him from a pleasant nap. I gave him the numbers of the VW's Maine license plate and detailed my location. I was near the twenty-nine mile marker in Russell, Massachusetts, entertainment capital of the world.

Though everything seemed pretty routine, I was sure to mention that I was westbound, knowing that making a habit of that minor detail of procedure could save my life some day if I ever needed rescue or back-up. I turned the heater on and sat back, waiting while the dispatcher activated his teletype to run the Maine registration.

When the dispatcher came back on the air he was all business.

"M to 126—vehicle reported stolen from Hampton, New Hampshire. Believed operated by a wanted felon: James Hopkins. Believed armed and dangerous. Do you need assistance?"

Knowing my nearest help was probably in Charlton, about fifty miles distant, I declined a back-up. I told them I was all set, that the vehicle appeared to have been abandoned.

"You sure? this Hopkins is wanted for several robberies in Maine and New Hampshire. He's always been armed and has threatened to shoot more than once."

I said I'd continue the investigation solo, but promised to call in on the half hour. I headed west. There was a highway Hojo's service and rest area about five miles west at Blandford. I figured that whether the driver had mechanical problems or had simply abandoned the car, he'd want a pitstop to warm himself up in this weather, especially after driving a VW.

My eyes peeled, I glided through the parking lot of the darkened roadside restaurant to the bright, neon-lit service station. Nothing seemed out of order. The station attendant was alone. He had waited on my suspect.

"Young guy—gave me a deposit on a can of gas. Hitched a ride with an eastbound trucker." The attendant jerked his thumb back in the direction I'd just come from. "They just left; guy said he'd bring the can back."

I crossed over the wide median area and raced eastbound back down the mountain again, toward the VW. I hated like hell to call for assistance when I had no idea yet if this person was even the wanted guy.

Heading downhill on a straightaway, about a mile away from where I'd first found the abandoned VW, I spotted the car headed back toward me on the opposite side. Apparently refueled, it was slowly climbing back up the mountain westbound toward the New York border again. Cripes.

Zipping down to the next crossover, I made a quick U-turn and headed after him. If the guy in the VW didn't keep a straight line for a while I was going to get dizzy. Though several miles behind, catching the 4-cylinder bug was a no-sweat proposition for the big Chrysler gas hog. I was only slightly behind him when he turned in to the service area again. He had pulled up to the pumps and was talking to the attendant as I rolled in.

I approached on foot cautiously, going on the assumption that this guy was Hopkins, armed and dangerous. If he turned out to be someone else I could always apologize later. Alive, I could apologize.

"That your car?" I asked, pointing.

"Yeah, ran out of gas down the road," he said, handing the attendant back the gas can and looking sheepish. His voice was conversational and apologetic, but he was edging toward his car. If it was his car, then this had to be Hopkins, the guy who did robberies with guns. I couldn't take a chance on him getting to a concealed weapon.

"Hold it." I grabbed him by the shoulder, spinning him around, away from his car. As he spun, I aimed a boot at the back of his heels, using his own momentum to sweep his legs out from under him and bring him down. As he went down I brought one of his arms behind him and went down with him, landing hard on his back. Hopkins was squirming like an eel, struggling wildly, but I had the position advantage. I forced his other arm back and finished the cuff. He hardly knew what hit him.

The attendant stared at us, dumbfounded, not knowing what to do.

"Car's stolen," I said, yanking Hopkins to his feet.

The best the attendant could do was nod. He gawked at the prisoner and me as if afraid I'd shoot him. He'd probably heard a lot about police brutality in those years and thought he was witnessing one of his minding-his-own-business customers roughed up right before his eyes.

My prisoner cleared up any budding misconceptions.

"Motherfucker," he screamed, spitting out his rage, "I get to my gun—I'll *kill ya*, pig motherfucker!"

I hustled him over to the cruiser. Hopkins kept on screaming, only now from pain. He complained I'd secured the cuffs too tightly, that they were crushing his wristbones. The way he begged me to loosen the cuffs, he sounded like a little crybaby. I checked. They did look a trifle snug.

While catching my breath, I thought about letting him yelp for a while, not feeling too kindly toward him for his recent outburst regarding my sexual preference. But I relented, mostly because I couldn't stand to hear him screaming all the way back to the barracks.

After a careful body-search and ID check confirmed this was indeed Hopkins, I loosened the cuffs and strapped a suddenly quiet and grateful prisoner into the front passenger seat. All his aggression seemed to have suddenly melted out of him. I couldn't tell if the sudden mood swing was due to gratitude for a small favor, or manic-depression. I'd seen stranger behavior, but Hopkins was throwing me a little curve now that he was subdued.

Besides his unexpected calmness, he had a clean-cut, all-American fifties look in an era when hippies with fright afros were too commonplace to cause comment. He was dressed like a conservative preppie; he just looked too harmless and innocent to be a crook.

If you asked a cop to describe an average armed robber, his description would not fit Hopkins. His ID said he was twenty-three. I'd more likely have picked him out of a line-up as a young college kid heading home for the weekend. In my experience, most armed robbers were typically from broken homes or raised by an abusive or alcoholic parent. They eventually steal their way into reform school, and in almost every case do their graduate work in a house of correction or state prison. I left my prisoner cuffed in the cruiser while I did a search of the stolen car.

The more I searched, the madder I got at Hopkins—but the more relieved I also became that I'd zapped him when he made a move for the car. I had moved rather hastily. Today's civil libertarians would rather I'd waited until Hopkins shot me. I'd be dead, but then I'd have established probable cause for laying a finger on him.

In the pouch pocket of the driver's side door I found a snub-nosed Smith and Wesson .38 with five live rounds chambered. Guess what Hopkins had been going for? A further search yielded a bunch of hypodermic syringes and a handful of glassine bags of white powder. The susbstance would have to be laboratory-analyzed for court, but I'd bet my badge it was heroin. The discovery of the drug helped explain Hopkins' high-low behavior. My guess was that Hopkins wasn't high at the moment but hadn't reached the itchy stage either.

Coming back to the cruiser I could hear all kinds of radio activity, most of it aimed at me. The dispatcher's voice was rising, showing a little anxiety. I quickly grabbed the mike, realizing he was worried because I'd overshot my promised half-hour call-in. I assured HQ that everything was under control.

"126, M. Subject under arrest. Vehicle at Blandford rest area, I'll proceed to Westfield with prisoner."

Sounding relieved they didn't have to send the mounties, HQ filled me in with new information received on Hopkins.

"Looks like he's a junkie, 126."

"Tell me about it."

"Five armed robbery warrants out for him. He did a 7-11, a MacDonald's, a Burger King and two drugstores—all on the same weekend," HQ said. All warrants were from New Hampshire and Maine.

"Figures," I said, looking at Hopkins." I found drugs and a weapon. He fits the bill."

I left instructions about the VW with the attendant and headed east on the pike with my prisoner. The adrenalin was wearing off now and I was feeling gratitude for what could have happened but didn't. We'd driven several miles before Hopkins broke the silence.

"Thanks for loosening the cuffs, the pain was killing me, honest," he said. He paused, his face working through a range of emotions as though he was finding it difficult to speak, then continued. "And I'm glad you caught me."

"Glad, why?" He'd caught *me* off guard.

"It was only a matter of time before I killed someone," he said clearing his throat. "I'm sure of it. You saved me from killing somebody."

Maybe even me, I thought.

Hopkins was in a confessional mood. With little prodding from me, he began telling me his life story. In keeping with his non-criminal appearance, his background was not stereotypical. He'd had a happy, uneventful home life as a child. He was the Hollywood version of the boy next door. He was never in trouble. In high school he'd been an A student, class officer and all-state halfback on the football team. Handsome and outgoing, he was popular with all his classmates. At graduation from Hampton High, great things were predicted for James. Awarded a full scholarship to Columbia, he had the world at his feet. Until he started fooling around with drugs.

"I never thought I could get hooked. Me? I was too smart," Hopkins said. He had drawn a believable and fascinating word picture of the irresistible allure of New York City to a kid on his own after leaving tiny Hampton, New Hampshire. "The twenty-four-hour excitement is what got me at first, then the idea of acting sophisticated in front of what I considered jetsetters, with marijuana and pills. At first I thought I was just dabbling around, using a little here and there, but it must've amounted to a little more than that because by the next year, my sophomore year, I was already mainlining heroin."

I nodded in sympathy. "Follow the yellow brick road."

" 'Zactly," Hopkins said. He began scratching himself, doing the best he could with cuffs on. At first it was as if he was after a mosquito bite. "Except I didn't even stop at Go to collect my two-hundred dollars, me—the smart guy. Hooked. Columbia flunked me out and I was back in New Hampshire with a solid habit before I knew what was happening. A junkie. Stealing to support my habit." Now he was scratching with more fervor, displaying some of the earlier signs of withdrawal.

"That you?" I said, gesturing at the radio. "You do all those jobs they said?"

"Yours truly," he said, expelling air. "You should've seen their faces when I pointed my gun at them. The truth is, I was probably a lot more scared than they were. But I don't know what I might've done, eventually. How far down I might've gone. That's why I'm glad you stopped me. Before I did something to really shame my folks. They already disowned me."

Hopkins revealed he was on his way to Chicago when I intercepted him. He assumed going there would remove the embarrassment of his criminal life from his parents. He also stated he hadn't had any dope for three hours.

"I'm getting a little frazzled," he said, his voice shaking and his spastic eye and hand movements showing increased withdrawal symptoms. "You think I could get a fix?"

"What kind?" I asked, as if I didn't know. It was a kinder way of telling him there wasn't a chance of him getting any drugs from me. Without saying the words, it let Hopkins know I knew he needed a fix, but that no amount of pleading was going to get an illegal one out of me.

"Sugar," he said "Could we stop somewhere for a candy bar? Just something to take the edge off."

My patrol supervisor had driven out from the barracks and met us at the Westfield interchange. He left his cruiser there and joined the prisoner and me for the ride to the Westfield Police Department. If felt good to get off the interstate and onto some local roads for a change.

"Nice job, Dave," the sergeant said, eyeing my prisoner. "Looks like a kid. Had a gun in the car, eh?"

"Snub-nosed .38," I answered. Spotting Doc's Smoke Shop just as we got to Westfield, I pulled the cruiser over. "Be right out. Gotta get a couple of candy bars."

The sergeant looked at me like I was a little weird but shrugged his reluctant approval. I know he thought the candy was for me. I could hear his mind clicking over, registering my tastes as somewhat unmanly for the trooper image. But what could he say—after I'd just subdued a wanted, armed criminal? I mean, John Wayne would have gone for a shot of redeye, but we weren't allowed to drink on duty.

Inside Doc's, the early risers were purchasing morning newspapers before the daily commute. Doc smiled, ringing up my purchase of several candy bars. Going back to my own youth, I bought my heavy favorite, Snickers.

"Shouldn't eat so much candy, Trooper," Doc admonished in his Yankee drawl. "Could be addictive."

"Know what you mean," I said, looking past Doc out the plate-glass window to my prisoner shaking in the back of the cruiser.

"I'll try to keep it under control."

Author near Lee Barracks, 1965

From left: Daniel Twomey, president of the State Police Association of Massachusetts; Edward King, former governor of Massachusetts; and Frank Trabucco, commissioner of the Massachusetts State Police

Graduating class, State Police Academy, Framingham, Massachusetts: Frank Trabucco and Deputy Superintendent James T. Canty in civilian clothes; author in front row, second from right

A "55 Team"—a federally funded unit created in 1975 to enforce the 55 mph speed limit

State Police Armorer Sergeant Bob Goldman showing recruit Ann Kelleher how to operate a gas gun

Author's entrance exam at Boston Garden, January 23, 1962

South Boston housing project at the height of the busing controversy

Recruits double-timing to meal formation

Instructor Laura Beurman overseeing P.T. test at Framingham Academy

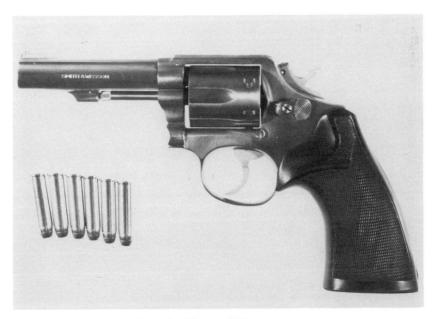

Standard issue .357 magnum

Author and Captain Robert E. Dunn standing at attention during academy graduation at Commonwealth Armory, Boston

Author standing in front of scuba team van

Author after apprehension of the Ramsland

State Police Academy, Framingham, Massachusetts, late 1950s

Academy staff

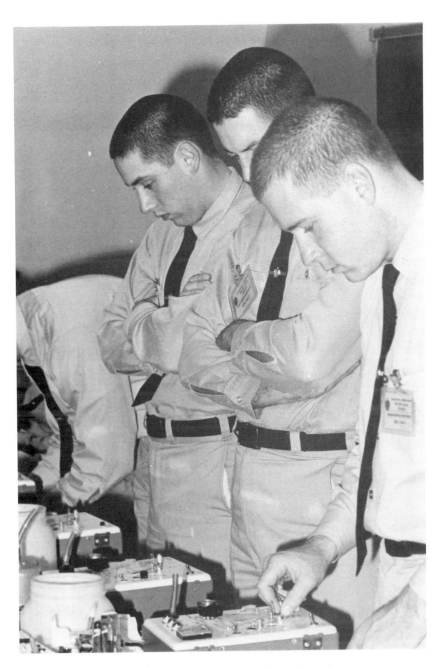

Recruits learning to operate a breath analyzer

Troopers and attack dogs

Troopers in riot gear in South Boston

Trooper Albert Balestra with guns, 1.5 kilos of cocaine and $60,000 cash, seized after an undercover investigation

Author and scuba team searching for a body in Boxford, Massachusetts

Staff Sergeant David W. Moran

11. The Brothers Grim

Hey, drinkin's no crime...

Time: 1970s
Location: Adams District Court
Duty: Prosecuting officer

It is hard not to find at least one person, even in the most cynical segments of society, who isn't willing to believe there is some good in the worst of us. Media moguls, including moviemakers, are as naive or gullible as the rest of us, giving even Frankenstein's monster a spot of humane softness, at least when it comes to little blond girls. Who could be so utterly unromantic as to harbor the belief that there is a portion of society that doesn't have some redeeming human attributes?

Cops—that's who!

Law enforcement officials are among the few people on earth totally convinced there is such a thing as a wholly evil person. Conversely, they are also among the first and loudest to expound the theory that many of the supposedly worst examples of humankind aren't really all that bad if they get to be known as people separate from their records. So their opinions have credibility, since they have met criminals who are totally irredeemable and can cite firsthand encounters as examples.

I definitely encountered people who are an affront to the rest of humanity. Behaviorists and academicians may account for their antisocial antics in a logical, dispassionate, detached style, but take them out of the sterile classrooms and put them face to face with one of these psychopaths—then see how they react. More than once in my career I've come across individuals who are simply evil—individuals who would consciously choose evil over good and commit evil acts without a second thought. I believe they never suffer a twinge of conscience because they don't own a conscience.

My personal worst list would have to be topped by the Andersen brothers of Plainfield, Massachusetts. Edward Andersen, older than his brother Albert by a year, was the role model in their quest for quintessential rottenness. Like the proverbial minister's children who turn out to be the town's worst sinners, the Andersen brothers were the offspring of the owner of a local garage who also served as police chief.

There was never much doubt which way the boys were headed. They were noticeably behind their contemporaries in school, although considerably larger physically. The difference in size from their peers increased as they were kept back to repeat several years. Young Albert completed the eighth grade and received his driver's license the same day. Minimum age to drive in the Commonwealth is sixteen. The role model, Edward the Elder, set the family's educational style by quitting high school in his freshman year to join the army. Albert followed, enlisting a year later.

Tolerant the army is; crazy it is not. The brothers Andersen were soon dismissed with dishonorable discharges and, I imagine, a sigh of relief. The military had put up with a series of thefts, arrests for intoxication and assaults on superior officers. The suspicion lingers that had they only been charged with theft and drunkenness they'd never have run afoul of the armed service. But the military does frown darkly on anyone tampering with their commissioned gentlemen.

The Andersens returned to their Berkshire birthplace none the wiser for their experience and landed jobs as hands on a large potato farm. It didn't last long. No job did. Their imposing size and natural strength suited the Andersens for almost any employment in the heavily farmed Berkshire and Connecticut Valley regions, but their penchant for drinking-induced rowdyism coupled with chronic absenteeism meant they never held any job for long.

The Andersen brothers had become infamous with state troopers from the Pittsfield, Northampton and Shelburne bar-

racks by the time they'd reached their mid-twenties. Their hometown, Plainfield, was in the Northampton patrol area, but the
small towns adjoining Plainfield were served by Shelburne in the
north and Pittsfield in the west. Being equal opportunity troublemakers, the Andersens didn't limit themselves to just their own
hometown. Thus, they were well-known to troopers and other law
enforcement officials from all over western Massachusetts.

Their most recurrent offense was assault. Edward and Albert
had been arrested for inflicting physical mayhem in barroom
brawls in almost every hill town in the Berkshires. They also managed to get grabbed for various larcenies and motor vehicle violations, but beatings were their specialty. Felonious assault. Typical
bullies, they usually chose a target they knew could be easily vic-
timized—usually old men, drunks and people smaller than themselves. They always worked in tandem. Despite the brothers' own
imposing size, large muscular young men were pretty safe from attack by the Andersens.

Interestingly enough, the insular nature and the singular communal morality of those small hill towns created an ironic attitude—the townspeople would just as readily blame the victim for
getting involved with the Andersens as they would the brothers for
committing the crime. That perception certainly contains elements
of common sense, and I can see the Yankee scrabble-for-a-living
morality in there—but still, how do you blame the *victim* in a
murder?

The following strange event began not with me, but with a
friend and fellow officer, Trooper John Bendonis. On a misty fall
afternoon Trooper Bendonis was radio-dispatched to the North
Adams regional hospital: "Interview a beating victim," the dispatcher said. Bendonis was oblivious to the majestic oaks and
flaming maples as he sped down the tree-lined mountain roads
toward the hospital. Knowing the territory and the people in his
assigned patrol area was his specialty, and Bendonis was trying to
put a face with the name of the victim.

"The woodcutter," the dispatcher had said. "Stanley Wojieck,
you must know him."

"From Savoy, I remember the name," Bendonis answered, con-
firming the dispatcher's assumption. He vaguely remembered Wojieck the woodcutter as an older man, something of a loner. He'd

seen him at some of the local hangouts, always alone, and thought of him as unmarried, although he didn't know for sure. He recalled thinking Wojieck a somewhat pitiable figure.

Bendonis smiled wryly to himself as he headed toward the shrinking industrial town of North Adams. He knew he had pulled this assignment precisely because he was expected to know the victim—and probably everyone else domiciled within his patrol area. An ex-accountant, Bendonis was known for his meticulous attention to detail. They didn't call his daily notebook the Book of Kells for nothing.

Coming into the old mill town, Bendonis flashed past the Hoosac tunnel, once the only rail link between Boston and Chicago. This eight-mile tunnel through New England granite, hailed as an engineering marvel when opened in 1870, was now obsolete. The massive steel doors at either end were now guarded by silent watchtowers, installed in WWII as prevention against enemy sabotage. Rust was the only thing happening around the tunnel these days. The tone of desolation was matched by the abandoned paper and woolen mills that filled the decaying core of the city and lined the approach road to the hospital. It would be a while before redevelopment was a hot item in this neck of the woods. Bendonis was met outside the hospital by the Savoy Chief of Police.

"Took you long enough, John." Chief Earl Bates smiled to soften his sarcasm. He stuck out a hand of welcome to the tall, muscular trooper. Bates was actually only the part-time chief. Savoy wasn't big enough to demand a full-time force. Earl and his family ran a store and garage on Route 116 that was the hub of all social and commercial activity in Savoy and the surrounding region. He was a valuable man for a trooper to know.

"What we got here, Earl—someone actin' up in your bailiwick?" Bendonis asked. Like Bendonis in his patrol area, there was precious little that happened around Savoy that Chief Earl Bates didn't know about. Other than his establishment, two churches, a post office and a fire station made up the rest of downtown Savoy. Morning coffee in Earl's place was the most valuable source of both gossip and hard information in the entire area. That is, if you were accepted enough for the natives to talk in front of you.

Chief Bates shrugged. "Know 'bout as much as you boys in the pretty uniforms, officially. Until I talk to the victim. Got my suspicions, though," he said, leading the way into the hospital.

Bendonis accepted the good-natured ribbing and followed the chief. He smiled, remembering the long initiation period he'd suffered through and all the scheming it had taken him to achieve this seemingly easy acceptance. These western Massachusetts natives didn't open up to just every new city escapee from Lawrence or Dorchester. Especially if he worked for an official agency.

Because it was the recognized center for intelligence in the area, a trooper assigned to patrol Savoy would eventually try to ingratiate himself at Bates's store. Each new man would get the silent treatment for anywhere from a few days to months before some degree of acceptance was accorded him. A hundred cups of coffee on a hundred different days might be consumed before they'd receive even a perfunctory nod from the locals. Bedonis's case was different. He was accepted more quickly than most, but it had still taken him a while.

With the persistence inherited from his Lithuanian forbears, Bendonis had hung in there. From a working-class Worcester background, he had worked in a foundry and related well to the hardy natives. His quiet, polite manner quickly gained the respect and confidence of people in the new area. He solidified this confidence and built on it, moving to an adjoining town and acting and looking like a native when not on duty.

After several years working out of the Pittsfield barracks, Bendonis had stored up a reservoir of trust among the natives of the region. When calling to report a crime, people would ask for him by name. Barracks wags contended that some people would report *only* to him. According to one story, a caller, frantic to speak to Bendonis, was advised that John was away on vacation and couldn't be reached, no way, no how. Then, and only then, did the caller acquiesce. He reluctantly advised the desk officer that there'd been a horrible smash-up in Windsor and that people were bleeding all over the street—were they sure Trooper John Bendonis couldn't be reached?

So Bendonis was the right man to come to the hospital to interview the beating victim, Stanley Wojieck. The dispatcher at Pittsfield barracks, aware of John's status, was confident that the trooper would receive local cooperation. He usually assigned him to matters in this area and had always been gratified by his choice.

The dispatcher didn't have to worry about indiscretions or improper conduct that would reflect badly on the service.

A candy striper ushered Bendonis and Bates into the victim's room and then backed out self-consciously, as if aware she was on the periphery of exciting events. Her patient was either asleep or unconscious. Seeing the victim, Bendonis congratulated himself on recalling the correct person, the loner, the woodcutter.

Stanley Wojieck was a mess. He'd either been brutally beaten or he'd lost an encounter with a threshing machine. Wojieck had been a woodcutter all his life, an occupation requiring a strong body. It was evident that, bruises aside, this once powerful body had also been ravaged by age and alcohol and a lifetime of neglect. Bendonis guessed him to be in his early sixties. Wojieck's gray hair was still matted and streaked by dark blood from a nasty scalp wound. Both eyes were swollen shut over a face purpled with contusions.

As Trooper Bendonis and Chief Bates stood enumerating the bruises, a brisk young resident entered the room. He made notations on the chart at the end of the bed.

"Gentlemen," he nodded, acknowledging the two policemen. "The patient was admitted last night. Along with these obvious multiple cuts and abrasions, he has suffered several broken ribs and a broken collarbone."

The doctor affirmed that the injuries were positively from a beating, not from an accident—that was why the authorities had been informed. While talking to Trooper Bendonis and Chief Bates, the resident bustled around his patient—tapping here, lifting an eyelid there. He woke Stanley Wojieck. Introductions took place after Wojieck finished cursing out the thoughtless medico. The doctor left, suddenly remembering that another patient needed him. Wojieck was in severe pain, but his mind was sharp. He knew the chief and was familiar with the trooper. Shifting his lower body to ease the pain, he launched into his version of the previous night's assault, unequivocally implicating the infamous Andersen brothers.

"...Sonsabitchen Andersens," he concluded, the strain of the effort to speak showing on his face. He had been on what he thought was a night of friendly boozing with the Andersen brothers.

Despite their reputation for unwarranted violence, he thought he knew them well enough to sense if trouble were coming.

Chief Bates said, "Still doesn't make sense, Stanley. Why'd you leave the Stump with them in the first place?" The Stump was a notorious dive, the favorite watering hole of the local woodcutters.

"Seemed like a good idea at the time," Wojieck winced. "Like I tole you, I had the check money, and we was drinking it up."

"They were drinking on your money?" Bendonis broke in, surprised at these newly discovered facets of the Andersen's perfidy. Wojieck tried to nod but was prevented by the hospital apparatus for his severed collarbone.

"I was already in the Stump—feeling pretty good by the time they arrived—figured what the hell, buy 'em a drink, didn't expect to end up like this..."

"Can you remember what happened to your car?" Bates asked.

Wojieck reddened with impatience at our questions and the effort of retelling. "Uh-uh. Only thing I can say about the car is that after enough drinks we was all buddy-buddy and it seemed like a good idea to go spend some money somewheres else. All I can remember is driving the three of us to the Roadhouse.

"Somewhere in there, I ran out of money. After that, all I remember is being in the parking lot and getting the shit whaled out of me...Two of them, younger'n me, and bigger...I don't even remember getting here."

"Lucky they didn't kill you," Bendonis said. "Will you testify against them in court, Stanley?"

A light went on behind Wojieck's eyes. "Bet your ass!" he said.

The two policemen had heard enough. Promising action, they left Wojieck. The emergency staff established that the call for an ambulance came from patrons who had found the victim unconscious in the parking lot. The Andersen brothers had apparently fled the scene after administering the beating.

Chief Bates shook his head disgustedly. "Animals. Cripes, you'd think they'd call the old guy some help."

"Sure," Bendonis said. "Right after they prayed over him. I'll bet they even stole his car—which'll make finding them easier, the dummies."

Trooper Bendonis and Chief Bates left the hospital and separated, each promising to keep the other informed of their respective progress in the case, and to do their utmost to bring the vicious Andersens to conviction.

"Sad comment on humanity," Chief Bates said, getting into his Savoy Police car.

"We'll get them, Earl," Bendonis promised, confidently. "We've got indisputable testimony from the victim."

And he did, then.

As soon as Chief Bates left for Savoy, Bendonis headed south for the Adams District Court, where he sought warrants for the arrest of the Andersens. His tour had ended for the day, but he wanted to get to the court before they closed so he'd have the jump on the case if anything developed.

Appearing before the Adams District Clerk of Courts, Marc Trottier, the trooper swore out complaints on the Andersens. He made out papers for use of a motor vehicle without authority and assault and battery. He'd learned it's always better to have too much than too little when dealing in legal areas, where technicalities so often rob the arresting officer of justice. The clerk read over the complaints and warrant applications, immediately issuing warrants for the brothers.

Bendonis was up at dawn the next morning and out eagerly searching for the Andersens. From the barracks he cruised through Savoy, past the old town hall, and headed east on Route 116 toward Plainfield. Bendonis assumed that the brothers were smart enough not to be sitting at home waiting to be picked up. At the same time he knew the limits of their intelligence—they weren't smart enough to flee the area entirely.

He remembered the feelings of some of the people in the courthouse the previous afternoon, as well as the veiled remarks of Chief Bates. The townspeople were not so much angry at the brothers as embarrassed for their father, a good man who'd been in law enforcement himself. That embarrassment, however, wasn't stopping anyone from doing his job. The apprehension of the suspects was still priority number one.

Based on the victim's statement and all he'd been able to gather from his own informal grapevine, Bendonis figured that if the Andersens weren't outright alcoholics, they'd do until a real one came along. And where does one go to find an alcoholic? Where the booze is.

The trooper was putting his money on the hunch that they'd be sitting somewhere having a few drinks until the heat cooled off. Finding the Andersens shouldn't take a Sherlock Holmes. There were only two bars in Plainfield. John checked his watch, smiling. Both bars opened at eight in the morning. He was right on time.

In Plainfield, near the Savoy line, the Bass River Club is perched on a scenic bluff overlooking the swift-running, rocky-bottomed mountain stream that parallels the roadway. Bendonis entered with caution.

"Be my guest, Trooper, look around," the owner waved a bar rag at the bare tables of his empty barroom. "Ain't seen either one of the Andersens in over two weeks. Don't expect to, either. I doubt they'll ever be back, can't say I'm sorry about that."

"Why so?"

Bendonis knew the owner was alluding to a rumor, then circulating, that connected the State Police to this barroom. He hoped he'd supply enough data to give substantiation to what he himself had heard.

"Just a hunch," the owner shrugged.

Bendonis could see that was all he was getting from the Bass River Club. "Thanks, for nothing," he said, smiling, playing the game.

Back in his cruiser, the trooper recalled the rumor he'd heard in the barracks and on the street about a recent confrontation in this place. The Bass River was one of the boozing establishments favored by the Andersen brothers for local sprees. True to their pattern, they often taunted a fellow patron, itching to get a fight started, as long as it was someone they could handle. If they had no takers, they had to settle for brag stories describing who they'd do a number on, if only that person were there. Allegedly, when one patron threatened to call the authorities on them, their response was that they would "beat the crap out of the next state trooper they saw."

The rumor had it that the Andersens had been forced to eat crow during a confrontation in the bar. The situation was like something out of the Wild West. Ostensibly, an off-duty state trooper stalked to the Bass River Club with the avowed purpose of seeking them out. Supposedly, he'd faced the Andersens, arms spread to show he wasn't armed, and offered them out, saying, "Understand you two were looking for a trooper. Here's your chance, no badge."

It was said you could literally hear people breathing in the club, so eager were the customers to see the Andersens get their comeuppance.

The brothers loudly denied threatening the state trooper or anyone else and politely declined his invitation to continue their discussion in the parking lot. They were just a couple of good ole boys, out for a friendly drink.

Having called their bluff, the off-duty trooper left the brothers to the loud ridicule of the bar's clientele. An avalanche of abuse and horse laughter came the Andersens' way, released by the sight of them finally being faced down. The other patrons laughed the bullies out of the bar, tails between their legs. At least that's the way Trooper Bendonis remembered hearing it. When Bendonis tried to track down the rumor, each of his fellow officers in the Pittsfield barracks would nod as if they knew who the phantom cop was. Everyone said he was "well-known but unidentified." It seemed so widespread an opinion that he suspected no one knew for sure except the phantom himself.

Now Bendonis wondered if their humiliation added ferocity to the attack on Wojieck, or if it simply made it inevitable. He did know that if his investigation ever got hung up, he may have to interview a fellow trooper. If he ever found out who it was.

The Plainfield Men's Club was less than a mile from the Bass River. At this hour of the morning there were few cars in the unpaved parking lot of the roadside bar. The trooper ran a license check on one vehicle that matched the description given by the victim. Despite his own hunch, Bendonis was still surprised in the face of such audacity. Or stupidity.

It looked like the assailants had driven the stolen car to the local pub for some refreshment. The trooper entered the bar from a rear door. Incredible. The older brother, Edward Andersen, sat alone at the bar tossing down a few and chatting with the proprietor as if he were an ambassador on a goodwill tour rather than a suspect in a brutal assault.

Waiting until he was positive that Edward was indeed alone, Bendonis handcuffed him and advised him of his rights. Struggling, Andersen wanted none of it.

"Hey, drinkin's no crime!"

Bendonis told him what he was charged with.

"Wojieck's fulla crap! All I did was help the old guy. He was too drunk to drive, so I took his car so he couldn't kill himself on the road. He must've had a bad fall—that's how he musta got so bruised up. I din't do nothin' to old Stanley, my brother'll vouch for me."

"He'll get his chance," Bendonis said, hustling Edward out to the cruiser.

Two weeks later the trial of Commonwealth vs. Edward Andersen was held at Adams District Court. The state had decided its strongest case was against Edward. Eager for certain conviction against at least one of them, they figured their chances were better with the older brother this time. The court deemed Edward indigent, appointing an excellent attorney to defend him at public expense. The prosecuting officer for the Commonwealth turned out to be me.

My three years as a full-time district court prosecutor in Berkshire County gave me extensive experience in criminal work and a definite taste for trial work. This valuable trooper experience later motivated me to aim for a law career. I found the courtroom work extremely satisfying. Looking back now I can see why—it contained elements of many things that I enjoyed doing, like a chance to instruct.

Trial work satisfied my flair for drama. It also gave me a sense of really being able to direct the course of justice in some small way, on a person-to-person level. A legislator makes the laws but rarely sees them as a prosecutor does—as concrete rules that affect our daily lives. Like my police work, law gave me a feeling of being in the center of things. At any rate, it sent me to law school at Western New England College in my off-time and kept me there for the long haul.

All that's a long way from the Andersen trial, but it gives you an idea of the investment of time and heart that some of the dedicated people in our justice system put into the job. With all the disappointments inherent in a system that, in a democracy, is necessarily weighted on the side of the defendant, there has to be some attraction to keep people at it.

It was easy for me to throw myself into this case because I was so taken with the victim, Stanley Wojieck. My sympathy went out to a man who'd taken such a horrific beating primarily because of misplaced trust and an overriding need for human companionship. Wojieck never admitted it in exactly those words, but that was the essence I'd distilled from many hours of interviews and depositions.

A native of Plainfield, he knew the history of every family in the area, as any small-town New Englander would, semirecluse or not. Well aware of the nasty rep of the Andersen boys, he was a victim of the belief that "it'll never happen to me," deepened by his terminal loneliness. Bad company was better than being alone.

For his public defender Edward Andersen had one of the best attorneys west of Boston. He had no beef that way. As prosecutor in this nonjury criminal proceeding, I had the testimony of Stanley Wojieck, corroborated by evidence gathered by Trooper John Bendonis. As a negative benefit, I also had Andersen's lifestyle and a track record of proven misconduct. I was confident of the case I was bringing before Judge John Barry.

Judge Barry had a reputation for being firm but fair—high praise from law enforcement people and practitioners before the bar. I knew him as a compassionate, quiet man of even disposition, and I had a great deal of respect for him based on his work in the courtroom. The reason I felt so confident in the Andersen case, beyond the weight of my evidence, was the fact that Barry was a local product, an outstanding athlete and Pittsfield attorney whose only protracted time away from the Berkshires was as a Marine officer in the Pacific in WWII and as a student in law school at Georgetown. No matter how impartial he tried to be, I could count on his awareness of the overall evil repute of Edward Andersen.

The young public defender assigned to Andersen was putting up a good fight. But even through my bias I could see that the good guys were going to put his client away. My only question was how long a sentence. Following our presentation of the case, the judge motioned us to approach the bench. He never raised his voice.

"Gentlemen," he said, "I'd like to hear you both on final disposition."

I went first. I redefined the seriousness of the assault on Stanley Wojieck, making sure the judge got a good look at him. Even though his bruises were a couple of weeks old, the man's face still looked like hamburg. I delineated Andersen's past record of arrests, including other assaults, bearing down on the fact that he'd done almost no time behind bars because most previous sentences were probationary or suspended. Concluding, I pressed for the maximum sentence of two and a half years. Stressing that some time out of society was probably the only deterrent the defendant would comprehend, I finished with the dire prediction that if Andersen weren't put away now, he'd probably continue his reign of assaults until he killed someone.

The attorney representing Andersen tried hard. He made a strong plea for sympathy, trying to lay the blame on Andersen's upbringing, the rest of society and alcohol. These factors caused his client's problems in childhood, in the military and throughout life. Andersen attempted to compose a look of innocent interest during his attorney's summation.

Judge Barry quietly thanked both of us, then left the courtroom momentarily. When he returned he addressed Andersen, pronouncing him guilty.

"I'm sentencing you to two and one half years in the Worcester House of Correction. This sentence will be served. It is not suspended," the judge emphasized, while keeping his voice calm and even. "I'm in agreement with the Commonwealth's estimation that released to circulate in society, you might kill someone..."

The smug Andersen was stunned.

Everyone on our side felt that justice had been well served, even though brother Albert hadn't been charged. It looked like a happy ending to an otherwise horrible episode in the life of Stanley Wojieck.

Except that the defense attorney filed an appeal, and a superior court judge reduced Edward Andersen's sentence to ninety days. The warnings given by both me and Judge Barry were ignored.

Andersen was released in less than two months. On the street with a score to settle. To anyone familiar with the brothers Andersen it seemed like only a matter of time before my prophecy of murder would be fulfilled.

12. Some, You Just Have To Swallow

Out of the bathtub, into the hot water.

Time: Thanksgiving
Location: Back to the barracks
Duty: Coverage

Thanksgiving Day. It was about a month and a half after the successful appeal of Edward Andersen, and he was back on the street. I had been given a respite from my duties as court prosecutor and allowed to hold down the desk at the barracks while the sergeant enjoyed the day off. I didn't mind. Turkey Day is traditionally a quiet one in the police business. The day before is the most heavily traveled day of the year in the United States, but by the day itself people have arrived at their destinations and highway traffic has slowed down to less than normal. After the football games, folks head for the hearth to spend the rest of the day with family and food.

Due to the expected slowdown, only two patrols rolled from Pittsfield barracks that day, and everyone else had the day off. No one to bother us, I thought. I was watching the Lions-Bears game when Trooper John Bendonis called. Bendonis wasted no time with amenities.

"Just got a call from Chief Bates in Savoy, Dave. Stanley Wojieck was found dead in his bathtub yesterday."

"Saw that in this morning's paper," I answered "Article said heart attack. Guess the poor guy's out of his misery now."

"Yeah, heart attack. That's what the M.E. reported."

I detected sarcasm in Trooper Bendonis's voice.

"What's the problem John; why'd Chief Bates roust you on Thanksgiving?" I asked.

"The problem is, Edward Andersen is out of the correctional institute. Bates says he and his brother Albert were seen with Wojieck the day before his heart attack. He's even got a witness who puts the Andersens at Wojieck's house—"

"Where his corpse was discovered," I finished for my friend.

"Right."

I thought for a moment before I said: "But if there was anything unusual about the body, Dr. Kelly would've picked it up—wouldn't he?"

"Unusual? Like signs of a beating? Kelly's been the M.E. in these parts for about a hundred years, you'd think he'd spot something like that for sure, wouldn't you?"

"I'll check it out, get back to you." I hung up. In addition to Bendonis's concern, I had an unsettled feeling in my gut that said this case wasn't closed. So much for my quiet Thanksgiving and the Bears game.

I called in Trooper Larry Ashman from patrol to cover the desk. Ashman seemed glad to get in off the road for a while. Despite my sense of foreboding, I was delighted for the official excuse to be doing something besides sitting behind a desk.

Escaping from the barracks, I took the cruiser through the Coltsville section of Pittsfield and sped north on the holiday-empty Route 8. In Adams, Route 8 is also Main Street, which runs through the business district. A mile from the Adams District Court is Mitchell's Funeral Home. The morning newspaper had reported that Wojieck had been taken to Mitchell's from his home on the Savoy-Plainfield line. Heading there immediately, I had no worry about finding anyone working there on the holiday because the proprietors lived in an apartment above the funeral home and there were two wakes listed for that night.

Bill Mitchell, the funeral parlor director, evinced considerable surprise at my request to view the Wojieck body. He ushered me into the kitchen, away from the viewing parlors where the other wakes were being held.

"You're a little late, Trooper," Mitchell whispered with irritation. "We've already started working on the deceased. Heck, the guy's partially embalmed already."

"No problem, I only want to see his outsides, not do an autopsy."

He took me downstairs to his workroom in the cellar. I'd been there before, but that didn't make this trip any more pleasant. I didn't know what the partially embalmed body was going to do to my stomach.

Without preamble, Mitchell whipped the plastic undertaker's coverlet from the cadaver. Lifeless, Stanley Wojieck stared up at me from the gleaming stainless steel table. He looked like he'd been hit by a truck. His body was a mass of bruises and his face was discolored in several places, denoting trauma.

The thought that jumped out immediately was that he'd been beaten. Except for some differentiation in coloring due to this being a corpse, I imagined he looked much like Trooper John Bendonis had testified Wojieck looked when he first interviewed him in the North Adams Hospital after his beating by the Andersens.

"Did you do the removal personally, Mr. Mitchell?"

The undertaker seemed to resent my question. Before he'd answer, I had to reassure him I wasn't complaining about his embalming job. "Yes, I did," he said, finally. "My son and myself went to Savoy to pick up the body.'

"Who was there when you arrived?"

"His sister and a neighbor lady to keep her company."

"Nobody else? No spectators outside, anything like that?"

"That was it. Period," he said.

I bent close to the corpse's face, looking for marks and trying to determine how the bruises could have happened.

"Where was the body found?"

"Bathtub," he said.

"Had it been removed from the tub or was it in there when you arrived?"

"No, I removed it from the tub," Mitchell said. "The corpse hadn't been tampered with, Trooper."

"Must've been messy work," I sympathized, hoping to put him a little at ease.

"Not really. There wasn't any water in it."

"What! No water in the tub?"

"Bone-dry." The undertaker said.

At that point I wasn't sure what was going on, but I knew something wasn't kosher. The alleged manner of Wojieck's death was fishy. If Stanley died of a heart attack, then he must have fallen down forty-two sets of steps afterwards to obtain so many bruises. To have simply had a heart attack in his bathtub, and be in this condition, he'd have to have been sharing it with a school of man-eating sharks.

I also detected "a powerful odor of mendacity" from the funeral director, Mitchell. His nervous mannerisms and body language pointed to some kind of cover-up.

I found myself in one of the minor moral dilemmas that law enforcement people must solve on an almost daily basis. I sensed that Mitchell was covering up something—most likely a minor breach of standard procedure by him or his son, or even the medical examiner. Like Bendonis, I lived among these people. It's as important for state troopers as for anyone else to get along with their neighbors. In the rural ethic of the somewhat socially isolated Berkshires of that time, one would be considered anathema if he told on a neighbor.

The structure of this code is such that the closer to home and family the person is, the worse the stigma is for telling. The social penalty for turning in an unknown town inhabitant may be mild ostracism, but to tell on a family member demands a penalty geometrically escalated to the point where it might be better to move away. The only time this ethic does not apply is when the relative is an immediate social menace, like a serial killer. Even then it would matter whether he was killing neighbors or strangers—like people from Boston.

Regardless of the social consequences, I had an obligation to get to the bottom line here and determine what was going on. If it were merely a minor breach of some unimportant procedure, Mitchell could rely on my discretion not to blow the whistle. But if there was a cover-up of something serious, I had an oath to uphold that transcended village protocol.

Employing a subtle combination of tact and pressure, I got a new version of the events following Wojieck's death from Bill Mitchell. Doctor Kelly, the County Medical Examiner, contrary to state-mandated medical procedure following a death, did not examine the body of the deceased at the site of the death. Mitchell said that when he arrived for the removal and found the M.E. hadn't been there yet to issue a death certificate, he called Dr. Kelly. Tied up, Kelly asked if he could meet Mitchell at his funeral parlor instead of the death scene.

In spite of the unusual nature of the request, Mitchell said, he didn't want to alienate a highly respected local physician. After all, he was the M.E. and Mitchell had to work with him in the future.

"Besides, Doc Kelly was Stanley Wojieck's own personal physician like he was to half the rest of this neck of the woods. He should know what he's doin'," Mitchell protested. "All he wanted to do was see the body here instead of there. Wasn't like Stanley'd been in a shooting incident, or something like that."

"You didn't question how he got all those bruises?" I asked.

"I just transport them, I don't give them physicals." Mitchell finished by telling me that Dr. Kelly did indeed meet him at the funeral parlor and called his report to the D.A.'s office, standard procedure, listing Wojieck's death as heart failure.

I knew there was no follow-up from the D.A.'s office: both because the doctor had complied with standard procedure, and because the name Stanley Wojieck would mean nothing in particular to the staff there. They wouldn't respond to a routine heart attack.

That did it for me—that the M.E. didn't examine the body at the scene was not only gross circumvention of official procedure, it was uncommonly bad judgment. I had to blow the whistle. For all I knew, the doctor himself could be covering for someone. Anything was possible at this point. Kelly could be reporting a heart attack to cover up a beating. If so, I had a pretty good guess who might have administered it. I got on the phone immediately.

I called the D.A.'s office first. Finding Sergeant White on duty, I inveigled him to come to the funeral parlor. Then I called Kelly. The doctor wasn't at all pleased to be called out on Thanksgiving, but I convinced him it was imperative. And of course I called Trooper John Bendonis. He was the only one I gave any details to.

While waiting for everyone to arrive, I asked Bill Mitchell to run through the events of the preceding day one more time. I wanted to see if I'd missed anything. He told pretty much the same story in pretty much the same sequence until he got to where he described Dr. Kelly meeting him at the funeral parlor instead of the death scene.

Mitchell was giving off those nervous signals again. Last time they meant he was straying from the truth. I chased that one around for a minute, trying to think what else he might be holding back on.

"Wait a minute—" I interrupted on sudden inspiration. "Did Dr. Kelly ever actually *see* this body?"

Mitchell hesitated. "Sure...he viewed the body."

I stared him down. The seconds stretched out.

"Look, Trooper, Doc's my friend. We both grew up in this town—played sports together fuhcripesakes in high school."

"And?"

Mitchell was squirming now. Knowing he was giving away the story, he was looking for me to let him off the hook. I wasn't budging.

"We went to the same college." He looked pathetic, shooting his last arrow. "We're married to sisters."

Somehow, I guess that was supposed to count for something, mitigating the lies he'd told about his handling of this case. I couldn't help but wonder how many others had been so miserably botched or covered up.

Bendonis was the first to arrive. He was as excited as I about the possibilities opening up. We barely had time to sketch out a strategy. Sergeant White from the D.A.'s office and Doctor Kelly arrived on Bendonis's heels. I invited everyone downstairs and immediately began questioning Dr. Kelly.

We were gathered around the corpse, which lay on the stainless steel table. Sergeant White questioned me with his eyes, wanting to know what the hell was going on. I discreetly signaled him to be patient for a couple of minutes, hoping the M.E. would realize by my pointed questions that the jig was up. He could clear this whole thing up with some truth.

I didn't ask him any sticklers at first, but Doc's bristling ill humor let it be known immediately that he didn't appreciate this whole business, especially having his authority questioned by two brash young whippersnapper troopers. I kept on him, bringing the questions ever closer to home.

"So Stanley here died of a heart attack, Doc?" I'd already established Kelly had been the woodcutter's personal physician.

"I've been treating Mr. Wojieck for a heart condition for some time," he said, impatiently. "Saw him only a few days ago, as a matter of fact."

It was time to lower the boom.

"Did you actually go to the Wojieck home to issue the death certificate, Doc?"

Kelly hemmed and hawed and cleared his throat a few times before answering. "Well, ah...actually I didn't go right to the house. I was, ah, busy in surgery—I *knew* him." The doctor's voice betrayed some desperation.

Sergeant White rolled his eyes. He'd had no hint of anything amiss and this admission was a shock. It was unheard of for an M.E. to certify someone dead without being there to view the corpse. Rare, too, to hear a doctor admit a mistake. White remained silent and let me continue.

"Doctor, what about these bruises and abrasions?" I said, gesturing to the corpse.

"Well, yes, there are quite a few. But they—he drank a lot. They could be the result of a fall, you know." He looked like a man walking backwards on a slippery log.

Bendonis looked up from a close inspection of the body.

"You think he could've *beaten* himself to death, Doc?" he said impertinently.

Kelly shot Bendonis a furious look. To keep himself from breaking up, Sergeant White now swung into action. He was, after all, representing the D.A.'s office, and as such held the rank and authority in this situation.

"Let's call the state pathologist's office, have them perform an autopsy," Sergeant White said quickly, eyeing Dr. Kelly. "Under the circumstances, I think it's warranted."

Dr. Kelly didn't like the suggestion, which questioned his competence and authority, but he realized that the district attorney's rep was also giving him a way to save face; no mention had been made of bringing charges against him. He grudgingly nodded his approval.

Mitchell the undertaker led us up from his grisly workshop, and we left Stanley Wojieck's body for the pathologist's knife.

The next day the state pathologist arrived from Boston. I had worked with Dr. George Katsas many times and found him to be an interesting person as well as an extremely competent pathologist. A medical student in Greece at the outbreak of WWII, Katsas had served as a medical officer in the Greek Army. When peace came he traveled to the United States for postgrad work in pathology and decided to remain here.

The pathologist's job is to determine the cause of death. Under typically convoluted Massachusetts law, he is subordinate to the medical examiner. The pathologist has the training, experience and expertise, but the politically appointed medical examiner, a licensed physician, has all the legal authority in his particular geographical area.

The laws of human nature decree that more often than not the pathologist is going to try to agree with the M.E. In this instance, I was confident that Katsas was his own man and would tell the truth as he saw it.

The same cast as the previous evening assembled in the funeral parlor. As he worked, Dr. Katsas described every move into a tape recorder, cutting with speed and precision. Sergeant White quickly excused himself for a cigarette. Autopsies weren't his thing.

First he made a Y inscision from the shoulders to below the navel to allow the retractor to expose the rib area and internal body mass. Dr. Katsas made pointed note of the recently broken ribs and attendant bruising. As Katsas poked around among the deceased's organs, I thanked God I'd been a fan of Errol Flynn rather than Dr. Kildare. Finishing, Katsas determined that the cause of death was indeed a heart attack, but not due to an arteriosclerotic condition. Stanley Wojieck, the Savoy woodcutter, had been beaten to death.

"Gentlemen," Katsas concluded, "You have a murder on your hands."

After Doctors Kelly and Katsas left, Sergeant White called his superior at the D.A.'s office, Lieutenant Wilson, apprising him of the autopsy outcome. Bendonis and I relaxed while they discussed what steps to take next. John and I suggested they immediately issue warrants for the Andersen brothers.

When Sergeant White returned, he said the D.A. had decided that since Bendonis and I had brought the case this far, they'd let us continue to its conclusion. I'm positive they granted us this concession because others in the establishment didn't want us to draw attention to the illegal premature certification by Dr. Kelly. There was an unspoken bargain between us that if we didn't mention Kelly's screw-up, a prosecutable offense and a potential source of great political embarrassment, we could have the job of going after the Andersen brothers.

It gripped both Bendonis and me that if it hadn't been for Chief Earl Bates's phone call, the certification of death by natural causes would have stood and we'd never have been alerted to the beating. But there was nothing to be gained by going after Dr. Kelly. And we felt he'd be more conscientious in the future with Bendonis and me watching over him. We were convinced his sins were arrogance, neglect and bad judgment rather than malicious intent. In no way did we think he was covering for anyone other than himself. He simply certified the death without viewing the body.

The Andersen brothers were nowhere to be found. We had reason to believe they hadn't left the area, but they were making themselves extremely scarce. While I poked around looking for them, John Bendonis did the all-important preliminary investigative work and deposition-taking that would be so vital if we ever got them to trial.

As quietly and methodically as he did everything, the ex-accountant went everywhere, interviewing everyone who would talk to him. Some troopers swore Bendonis even talked to the trees. John eventually came up with three of Wojieck's neighbors who said they had seen the Andersens enter Stanley's house several hours before his death. They could not swear what time the Andersens left, but their statements put the Andersens at the scene on the day of the crime.

"What I want to know is, what the hell was Wojieck doing anywhere within five miles of those animals?" I asked.

Bendonis shrugged. "Maybe woodcutters dig beatings," he joked. I'm not sure we ever found the right answer to my question. I certainly didn't like what eventually became the only plausible one.

Bendonis established a sequence of events: the sister discovered Wojieck's body in the bathtub and called the family physician, Dr.

Kelly. Kelly just happened to be the M.E. We knew from our tete-a-tete with Kelly that he was tied up in surgery. He called his brother-in-law, Mitchell the undertaker, and asked him to do the removal, telling him he'd examine the body at the funeral parlor. The Savoy Chief, Earl Bates, heard about the death at his store several hours later in the day. Acting on a hunch, he eventually called John, who called me. Which all meant that no one in an official capacity, save the undertaker and his son, had viewed the body at the scene of its demise.

It wasn't until a week after the funeral that John and I heard a rumor that Edward Andersen had been seen around his mother's home in Montague. The Shelburne Falls barracks troopers who had checked out the residence had seen no sign of either brother; nor could their local informants confirm the rumor.

After the father of the Andersen brothers died, his widow had sold their garage in Plainfield and moved to Montague, a small town across the famous Bridge of Flowers.

"Probably died of shame," Bendonis said sadly. John headed us down Black Brook Road in Savoy toward the Mohawk Trail in Charlemont. We had decided to take a ride out to the Andersen place and see for ourselves.

I rarely got the chance to ride in a cruiser as a passenger, so I took advantage of the opportunity to enjoy the late fall Berkshire mountain vistas. Another month and this road would be impassable except to motorized Cat or snowshoes. I was so into it I barely noticed the car that passed us going the opposite way.

"Guess who just drove by us?" John said laconically.

"I give up. Farmer Brown? J. Edgar Hoover?"

John was braking the cruiser to a slurring stop. "No—Eddie Andersen," he said, spinning the wheel.

I jerked upright, looking over my shoulder. Andersen's car was already out of sight. My partner was hooping like a loon at the surprised expression on my face as he spun the cruiser into a U-turn.

Accelerator mashed to the floor, we caught up to Edward the Elder at the other end of Black Brook Road and managed to pull him over by Parry's potato farm. Eddie Andersen was alone and none too happy to see his two favorite troopers. He waited behind the wheel as Bendonis and I approached from opposite sides. His ferret glance flitted back and forth between us as if he expected us to draw and fire on him. He was extremely jumpy, even for him.

Bendonis ordered him out of the car, spread-eagled him, then patted him down for concealed weapons before clicking on the cuffs.

"C'mon—I ain't done nothin'," Andersen complained.

"Driving after suspension," John replied, pushing him into the back of the cruiser. "You're under arrest."

We let him sweat there for a few minutes while John and I locked up his car and agreed on a strategy. By the time we climbed back into the cruiser, Edward was really sweating. He seemed even more jumpy than when we first stopped him, a good sign the questioning would be productive.

"You know you don't have to answer this, Eddie. This isn't about the driving thing here. I'd like to talk to you about another matter," I said, leaning over from the front seat as if we shared a secret between us.

"Sure, Dave. Glad to help," Andersen said, the very model of civic cooperation.

"Too bad about old man Wojieck dying," I said, matter of factly. I wanted my manner to convey the impression that I already had all the answers, and needed him only to confirm what I already knew.

Eddie Andersen tried to look surprised. "No kidding? Gee, I didn't hear about it, being out of town all week."

"Were you? That's odd, your brother Albert said you were here—in fact, he told us you killed Wojieck, said you beat him to death!"

Andersen nearly broke the cuffs in his panic. "That's a lie!" he screamed. "I never killed nobody! My brother's a liar—you guys *know* that." He was buying it.

"Bullshit—I got it all down here from your brother," I yelled back at him. Snatching some typed papers from the sheaf on my clipboard, I brandished them in his face as if they were a signed confession. "Albert gave us a statement. He said *you* beat Wojieck to death...and we believe him."

"That lying bastard. *He* killed the old man, I didn't. Believe me—I tried to stop him!"

Once Edward Andersen's pump was primed there was no stopping the flow, all aimed at his kid brother Albert. Andersen told us the story of Wojieck's death. Bendonis and I tried to look as if we knew it all ahead of time, but we were listening as raptly as if he were giving us the A-bomb formula. Our blindman's bluff had worked.

"We were drinking at a bar with Woj, the old woodcutter," he began. "When his money started running low, we went to the post office to see if maybe his check came early. He bought a jug, and after that we went to his house an' drank some more. My brother asked him for some money, but Stanley wouldn't give it to him. They argued for a long time, then Albert got tired of that and started punching him. I tried to stop it, but he wouldn't. Then the old man fell on the floor. We tried to wake him up but we couldn't, so we took his clothes off and put him in the bathtub so it'd look like he'd fallen taking a bath...then we took off out of there," he finished. "Honest, you guys gotta believe me."

"You sign a typed transcription of that statement you just made, we'll believe you," I said.

"Cuz it makes more sense than what my lying brother said, right? You bet I'll sign—the bastard!"

Bendonis got us to Pittsfield barracks in record time. We had Edward's statement typed, signed and witnessed and had him in a cell before the cruiser engine cooled down. We then went in front of the Clerk of Courts and asked him to set very high bail.

Armed with a xerox copy of Edward's damaging statement and some leads on Albert's whereabouts, we went looking for the younger brother.

Inside of two hours we were in a package store parking lot waiting for young Albert. Huge, gangly and frighteningly Neanderthal, Albert resembled TV's Lurch. When he'd been drinking, he took on an even more sinister look. He emerged from the store, his arms around a load of booze. We were happy to see him occupied.

In seconds we had him in the back of the cruiser. You could tell this wasn't his favorite position, but he seemed to be resigned to something coming down. This time we didn't have to bluff; we had his brother's statement. I related to him what his older brother Edward had told us about the murder.

Albert Andersen didn't deny that a murder had taken place, but he did deny the implications of his brother's story. I handed him the copy of the statement as a clincher. After a few seconds of uncomprehending staring I grabbed it back, realizing Albert probably was illiterate but wouldn't admit it. If there was one thing I'd learned from experience by then, it was the supersensitivity of the criminal ego. I pointed to Edward's signature.

"You recognize your brother's writing, don't you?"

The brute just stared at the paper in my hand. He had to either take my word or admit he couldn't read. His beet-red complexion showed he was obviously furious, but he wasn't responding.

"Nice big brother you got there, Albert. Accusin' you of murder. Real loyal family type."

Still nothing.

"We believe your brother," I goaded. "Just your style, you puke...beating up old men. How about taking a crack at John or me? Here—no weapons—we'll take off our belts, step in the woods. Or aren't we old enough for you?"

I'd gone about as far as I could. Andersen ignored my taunts, staring at the paper for long seconds. I was about ready to give it up when he finally bit.

"Dirty bastard—Edward? He was with me the whole time. He beat up on the old man, too!"

Bendonis and I were jubilant. We had our men—on their own admission. We had tricked the only witnesses to the crime into implicating themselves.

Until we had a signed admission by Albert, John and I could only communicate our jubilation by eye contact. We whisked him to a steno at the barracks, then took turns patting each other on the back.

The D.A. soon brought us back to earth.

District Attorney Bill Flynn was a good prosecutor, aggressive and articulate. His common sense approach to the law was appreciated by all of us who worked with him. He didn't make many mistakes. When he took on a case, it generally meant he was 99 percent sure he could win. Though it seldom came, a worried look shaded with sarcasm was an infallible signal of his displeasure. Which made the abrupt summons to Flynn's office the very day of our jubilation all the more ominous. He was displaying both.

"Great job, you guys," Flynn said. "Both the Andersen brothers are charged with murder."

It wasn't until the ensuing silence lengthened into eternity that I realized he was being sarcastic. He ran an agitated hand through his shock of red hair, another unmistakable sign.

"So who the hell do you think will testify in this case?"

He had us flat-footed, feeling very stupid. Bendonis and I had an embarrassment contest. In our rampant enthusiasm to put these scum behind bars, we hadn't noticed the obvious. Charging both Andersens with the murder left us with no material witness! No one, besides them, had left that house alive that day. The victim certainly couldn't testify and the defendants weren't about to testify against themselves. And no jury would convict on purely circumstantial evidence.

We believed that the brothers were equally culpable, but we were sure Albert had done the crucial, fatal damage. After lengthy debate among the team of prosecutors, it was grudgingly agreed we'd drop the charges against Edward and go with his testimony against his brother. Bendonis and I let Flynn arrange for Edward's release. We just weren't up to that.

Disappointed and still a bit sheepish over the way we'd blown the collar, Bendonis and I hit the American Legion Post for a few quick beers.

"Look at it this way, John," I offered philosophically, "we got the worst of the two, and Edward'll never be as dangerous without his brother."

"Right, and given their nature, we'll get them again for something else—" Bendonis said. "So how come I'm not happy?"

I didn't have an answer for him.

13. Busing

Have you seen the Globe today?

Time: December 1974
Location: South Boston High School
Duty: Enforce integration/busing law

Except for contingents at Logan International Airport, the governor's office and the headquarters of the Department of Public Safety, most state police assignments in Massachusetts are strictly to outlying rural areas. Consequently, city-dwellers in the Bay State seldom have any personal contact with state troopers. Unless they have problems on an interstate or happen to hit one of the drunk-driving roadblocks, most urbanites never see a trooper, except in a parade.

Imagine, then, the surprise of residents of South Boston when they awoke one December morning in 1974 to find five hundred state troopers clad in riot gear, positioned on their neighborhood streets.

Racial trouble had long been brewing in the Athens of America. With its several major universities, Boston was considered the foremost seat of higher education in the land, a bastion of enlightened liberalism. Its leading newspaper, *The Boston Globe*, was unabashedly liberal in perspective and reportage. Many people around the country saw the city as being populated exclusively by well-educated liberals and radical students. That stereotype ignored the larger stratum, a solid core of blue-collar, working-class people of various ethnic backgrounds who populated the city's neighborhoods.

In many ways as insular and isolated as any Berkshire mountain community, the several ethnic neighborhoods of Boston were interested in maintaining their status quo. The school system reflected the neighborhoods in racial make-up. Black kids went to schools in neighborhoods populated in the main by other black kids. White kids went to the schools in their own largely segregated neighborhoods, with a resultant preponderance of whites in the student body. And successful school committee candidates got elected on platforms that promised to perpetuate the status quo.

That was the situation prior to 1974, the year a group of concerned parents predominantly, but not exclusively, black, believing that the quality of education in the black neighborhood schools was not as good as that in white neighborhoods, petitioned the federal court. They asked that the Boston schools be integrated in accordance with recent Supreme Court decisions regarding racial balance.

Federal Judge W. Arthur Garrity was appointed to the sensitive post charged with compliance. Judge Garrity placed the Boston school system in federal receivership and set out to achieve racial balance in the school population by cross-busing kids out of their own neighborhoods to schools in other neighborhoods. This plan may have looked good on paper, but for the majority of those who had to live it, it seemed pretty absurd to take a child out of the school near his house and bus him to a different school across the city.

Parents of both black and white children expressed fear for children bused to neighborhoods where they were not wanted. Groups sprang up to protest the court order by marching, demonstrating and picketing. Neither side's moderate majority seemed happy with either the problem or the proposed solution, and extremists on both sides added fuel to the fires.

The neighborhood of South Boston was chosen as the pilot sector for forced integration. Geographically, South Boston is a peninsula, with the inner harbor on one side and the outer harbor and ocean on the other. The shore of the inner side is heavily industrial; the outer is lined with public beaches. Between the two lies the tightly packed residential area proudly known as Southie.

During the summer preceding the 1974 opening of school, there were several racial incidents on the public beaches. Tension ran high as September approached. Fiercely proud, sensitive to the perceptions of outsiders, people in Southie sometimes overreacted, giving racial overtones to what was simply normal human intercourse.

The residents of Southie were incensed that their neighborhood was chosen first, ahead of East Boston or Charlestown, to implement Judge Garrity's plan. Southie considered its schools to be integrated anyway; the reason there weren't enough blacks in the schools to meet Garrity's arbitrary quota was that few blacks lived in Southie.

Trouble brewed in other sections of the city as well. Charlestown, another predominantly blue-collar Irish neighborhood, knew their turn was coming. Home of "Old Ironsides" and Bunker Hill, Charlestown is also notorious for its rough project area. Historically independent, Charlestown's people resented the federal government intervening. In other neighborhoods like Roslindale and Jamaica Plain, the potential for disturbance was an unknown, but there was never any doubt about East Boston.

East Boston is as Italian as Charlestown is Irish. Eastie is home to Suffolk Race Track and Logan Airport. Separated from downtown Boston by the harbor, its main access is by tunnel under the harbor. The tunnel not only carries heavy traffic to and from the airport, it also serves as the main road link to several communities north of the city. Police intelligence experts reported that the people of Eastie would blow up the tunnel before they allowed busing in their community. Some Southie residents believed Judge Garrity's decision to begin in their back yard was influenced by his fear of the vital harbor tunnel being blown.

By summer's end, the wildest rumors and most absurd speculations were receiving as much credence as fact. Opening day in September brought national media attention to the Boston school system, South Boston in particular. The media focused on the yellow school buses full of kids, and the formidable police presence.

The entire complement of officers of District 6 of the Boston Police Department was supplemented by the Tactical Patrol Force, a police force composed of volunteers from throughout the city. The TPF received special training in the riot control and civil disobedience work so necessary in the sixties, as well as special crime work. Outfitted in blue coveralls, combat boots and riot helmets, the TPF became a symbol of oppression to the residents of South Boston. Especially during the early part of the busing crisis, the TPF received the lion's share of media attention. As a result, much of the anger expressed by the people in those early days was directed at the TPF.

In their angry response to federal integration measures, some South Boston residents were indistinguishable from the stereotypical Southern redneck. TV camera crews and other media people, especially *Boston Globe* reporters, were often given rough treatment by the crowds. Despite police escorts, the buses bringing black children into South Boston from Roxbury were stoned. Students—black and white—attempting to enter school were taunted by residents held back by police lines.

There is no defense for racism, but the residents of South Boston did have their home turf literally invaded by forces that their tax dollars financed.

Inside the schools, although there was always a percentage of mature, responsible students willing to get along peacefully, fights broke out during every classroom change, regardless of the number of police officers stationed in the school corridors.

The students themselves were under immense pressure from outside influences. In addition to the learned prejudices of their home environment, the kids were receiving heavy doses of peer pressure. And, for the ones susceptible at that wanting-to-be-considered-grown age, there was considerable adult pressure. The students were bombarded by adult influences and opinions: from the people behind the police lines to adults casually met on streetcorners to opinions they heard expressed on TV.

Left simply to run its course, with the fights petering out as kids learned to get along and get back to business, human nature might have handled the integration less violently. As it was, the continuing tone of violence was pretty much set by outsiders and exacerbated by media attention.

The media sometimes create news by their coverage of it. Reporters seek drama. And what teenager can resist, if he knows he can be on the six o'clock news simply by taking a swipe at a kid of a different color? Or sometimes just standing around, screaming whitey or nigger. Remember too that these weren't preppies from Phillips Exeter; they were tough city schoolkids with plenty of experience in classroom violence before any racial issue evolved. In any case, the local cops, teachers and administrators had a serious problem on their hands. Much has subsequently been said and written about the stress suffered by the police who monitored busing and the toll was admittedly high, but hardly any mention has been made of the incredible strain put on the teachers, system-wide. The cops at least had weapons and riot gear. The teachers were on the front lines too, and they were unarmed. And things got worse.

The violence, especially inside the schools, escalated as the months wore on, climaxing on December 12, 1974, when a white student, Michael Faith, was stabbed by a black student at South Boston High. Word of the incident spread like wildfire from the first students out of school to the local Southie residents. An angry crowd was soon surging around the school, feeling that their worst fears were being realized.

The Boston Police were barely able to contain the shoving, cursing, stone-throwing mob. When the police were finally able to get the black students safely on the buses and out of the area, school administrators decided to close for a few days to let things cool down. The Boston Police weren't convinced they could maintain order when school reopened, with only their own resources at their command.

Judge Garrity huddled with the police and school officials. Help was needed. The Boston PD was spread dangerously thin. Everyone was on full overtime trying to handle a regular workload in addition to the busing at Southie and elsewhere. By now Hyde Park and Charlestown High Schools were also included in the busing agenda. The decision was made. "Call in the State Police."

One stipulation of the decision to call us in was that there be no advance publicity. I was at home when the call came at ten o'clock on a Wednesday night. Brief message: report to the academy in Framingham next morning at 0500 hours. A former high school English teacher, I was heading back to school. Only this time no books or lesson plan, but helmet, gas mask and riot baton.

After a lousy three hours sleep I was on the Mass Pike headed toward Framingham and the academy, a hundred miles east. Around Sturbridge and Springfield I first noticed another B Troop cruiser heading in the same direction. The farther east I traveled into the increasingly heavily populated sections of the state, the more cruisers I saw—a small hint of the size of the operation to come.

My blood quickened as I waved back to the various troopers passing me in their cruisers in the predawn darkness. I imagined that in a small way this was how D-day or other large military movements must have felt to GIs.

I arrived at the academy in an hour and a half. It was crawling with troopers. There were cruisers all over the place, hundreds, and a herd of big Mass Bay Transit Authority buses.

We weren't allowed inside to disturb the cadet class. Our troop officers and NCOs quickly formed us into groups and loaded us onto buses. I was jammed into an aisle seat amongst about forty other half-asleep, grumbling, but excited men from B Troop. I was swapping stories when Lieutenant Ashe jumped aboard yelling my name.

"Moran, where's Dave Moran?"

I raised my hand so he could see me.

"You were stationed in A Troop weren't you, Moran?"

A was the troop assigned closest to the city of Boston. I indicated I'd had that distinct honor before being assigned to B Troop.

"Good—get your cruiser. B and C are going in first. You're going to lead us in. Don't get us lost."

Catcalls following me across the parking lot, I retrieved my cruiser. Reveille blew for the cadets. The lights came on in the billets as I cranked up the car again. At least it was warmer and roomier than the bus.

Our troop commander, Captain Winthrop Doty, joined me in the front seat. Doty was a tall, easygoing guy. He gave me orders to lead out the convoy at precisely 0600 hours.

"Get us on the Mass Pike at Natick, Dave," he said. "The eight buses will follow us all the way in."

"All the way where?"

"Bayside Mall, South Boston. Hope the hell you know where it is—none of *us* do, this is like foreign territory."

The captain was referring to the fact that B and C Troops were far from the Hub. He was also making the small-towner's universal assumption that because I'd been assigned to Boston for some undercover work, I would know every nook and cranny of the city.

"No problem, Cap'n," I answered, sounding a lot more confident than I felt. I knew he didn't want to hear indecision. Oh well, go down in a blaze of glory. I just hoped that when we got close to the city I'd see some landmarks that would perk my memory. In my mind's eye I could see me missing the turnoff and leading eight busloads of troops from central and western Massachusetts down the southeast expressway toward Cape Cod while all the brass hats fumed back at the assembly area.

The order came at 0600. "Move out."

The early commuters craned their necks at the eight black, smoke-belching monsters in convoy. They'd slow at the sight of the cruisers and hang back until they realized they were escorts, then they'd whizz by. The December sun still hadn't risen as we neared the lights of the city's tall buildings.

I started getting nervous after we'd swung south off the pike onto the expressway. Now, which exit was it? Was it Albany Street or Columbia Circle? I flipped a mental coin and took Columbia Road, which swung us back under the ex-way. I spotted the Old Colony Police Station and the Bayside Mall, our destination. Nothing to it.

The mall parking area was even more jammed with cruisers than the academy lot had been. What I didn't know at the time was there were a total of five hundred troopers assembling for day one of desegregation duty for the State Police. This contingent represented more than half our total complement—we're mandated by the legislature to have a thousand-man force, but because of budgetary shortages, the number is seldom higher than nine hundred.

Other troops continued arriving. Before we were assigned actual duties, it was like old home week. For twenty minutes we roamed around, greeting old friends we hadn't seen for years. Classmates found each other by noting the ID number stencilled on helmets. My class, for example, the Forty-Fifth Training Troop, had numbers from 657 to 705 in the table of organization chart. Because of assignment differences, some of the guys I hadn't seen since graduation day. One of my classmates ironically recalled that our graduation was December 12, 1962—twelve years ago to the very day!

The reunion was soon over. The NCOs' whistles formed us by troop into large military formations. Specialists, headquarters personnel and detectives unused to uniforms were also formed up. It was the largest single deployment of troopers in the history of the State Police.

As the sun rose over Boston Harbor we were hustled back onto the MBTA buses for the short shuttle to South Boston High School. The school overlooks the harbor from the top of a hill—not a bad view if you weren't on this kind of duty. Others from B Troop and I were redeployed down Sixth Street, a block from the high school, to the Hart-Dean Annex. By 0700 hours everybody was in place and expecting the worst. It was the first day of school after the Michael Faith stabbing.

Fortunately, the worst didn't come. Not that morning, anyway. People seemed to be staying home. The morning's buses came and went at the annex without incident. In fact, no threats of incidents. The streets were nearly deserted. Except for an occasional dirty look, the few people about seemed to ignore us deliberately, as if they didn't notice us in riding breeches and polished boots standing guard at their school.

We settled down to a few hours of anticipated boredom until the kids broke for lunch. An elderly man who had come out to pick up his newspaper in front of his brick row house on G Street was out again sweeping his steps in the cold morning sunshine. I struck up a conversation with the old tad. It turned out he was from very near where my family had come from in county Kerry, Ireland. My name in Irish is Daithi Liam O'Morain. The guy lit up like a Hanukka bush when I pronounced it correctly. Baile na Gael, where my people had emigrated from, is in the Gaeltacht on the Dingle Peninsula in Kerry, one of the last parts of Ireland where Irish is spoken. My Irishness established me with the old-timer as being within the human race, so he became willing to talk.

"You see no one on the streets now, do you now?" he said. "They'll be a few days comin' out. Afraid, they be."

"Of what?"

"You state boys," he said. "You're the ones who go into the prisons and beat up the niggers aren't you?" He spoke of some well-publicized instances where our men were used to quell prison disturbances. In his prejudice, he assumed anyone in prison was black.

"We didn't beat anyone. We put down a riot—" I tried. "And everyone in prison isn't black." He wasn't listening. He had already launched into a rehearsed diatribe against Judge Garrity and busing. I wondered how anyone like that could ever be reached.

I crossed to the mom and pop store on the corner across from the annex to get a newspaper. The store-owner looked up briefly as I entered, then went back to splitting chickens. It might have been my imagination, but I swore his cleaver was landing harder with every blow. The customers inside shot me looks that made me feel like a storm trooper occupying Holland. I'd have been happy to leave, but I couldn't find my paper in the display rack.

"Excuse me, any *Globes*?" I asked.

Except for the cleaver thunking into the butcher block, the silence was like High Noon. In the silence, light dawned on Marblehead. Innocently enough, I'd requested the liberal tagblatt that these people considered the instigator of the whole busing crisis.

"We don't carry *that* paper," the owner said, yanking the cleaver from where he'd buried it deep in the block.

"*Herald American* is fine," I said, pulling one from the pile. My back felt unprotected as I walked out. We had a ways to go in community relations.

We had lunch in the school cafeteria then waited for the buses to take the kids home for the day. The move was accomplished without major incident. Maybe our presence was having an impact? The brass tried to make sure.

Our contingent of troopers was marched from our position at the Hart-Dean Annex, up G Street to the high school where we mustered with the rest of B Troop. Once all the yellow buses had cleared the high school grounds, we were all assembled, five hundred strong. We were marched in military formation around the school, then down from the heights, along Telegraph Street to Dorchester Avenue. The route chosen was to expose us to a concentration of the local populace.

It was purely a show of force, a deterrent, to let everyone know we were there in strength—and our strength was awesome. We were marched to Dorchester Avenue to meet the buses as they finished their loop around Southie and to see them safely on. We lined up along on "Dot Ave" as the buses rolled by, out of Southie. I like to think it gave the kids on the buses some feeling of security to know we were there. Once the buses were gone, we were loaded back onto MBTA buses ourselves and taken back to Bayside Mall. There I picked up my cruiser and led the convoy back out to the academy.

Squinting into the setting sun as I headed back out the turnpike, I heard high praise on the radio news for the troopers during our day one in South Boston. It would be interesting to see how long our image remained heroic. I knew we already had orders to return at 0600 hours. I wondered how long we'd be committed as a unit to monitor school desegregation.

If anyone had said at the outset that it would be three long years before we left South Boston, I would've thought twice about finding the right exit on the expressway.

14. ...And Other Days

Hey Moran—how's it feel to be back in school?

Time: 1974
Location: South Boston
Duty: Busing

We weren't long establishing a routine, even amid the electrically charged environment of Southie High. We monitored the arrival of the buses in the morning; spent the school day on corridor duty, breaking up fights as they happened; and supervised the departure of the buses in the afternoon.

There were so many heavily armed men stationed around the school and its immediate environs, the scene resembled one of those old movies where the native army stands shoulder to shoulder, lining the hilltops all around. In our case, there actually was a trooper every five yards, inside the school and out. Believe me, in the beginning every one of those troops was needed. Just getting the kids from the buses into the school alive each morning was a major task. Early mornings, everyone was fresh and spoiling for a fight.

Fights were a constant inside the school. We had a flying squad assigned just for responding to classroom situations, but most of the action was in the hallways. Every time the bell signaling a shift of classroom rang it was like the gong signaling a new round of the old Friday night fights.

We troopers prepared for each change of class by donning our helmets, getting out riot batons and taking up strategic positions. We knew what was coming. Most of the fights were brief, but fierce, and of course we were always at risk, trying to break things up. The girls fought with the same intensity and even more decibels. More than one trooper caught a knee to the groin from some teenybopper who looked like butter wouldn't melt in her mouth. The fighters were both sexes, all sizes, all colors. The scuffles were usually continuations of some earlier gripe between kids of different color, with a brother or friend picking up the action as if in a Hatfield-McCoy feud. It wouldn't have been so bad if each incident were limited to just the initial combatants, but every single incident—whether it was a simple slap or an attempted stabbing—drew every available kid of both races. Even heated words led to what looked like bench-clearers in major league baseball.

Most fights started in the stairwells, which were the most difficult for us to observe or cover. And they'd usually end up in one of the lavatories. On occasion, one would start in a classroom and spill into a general melee out in the corridor. Whenever we could tell who started what, we'd take them to the guidance office where they'd receive suspension and be sent home.

Metal detectors had been installed at the schools after the Michael Faith stabbing. Each morning each student filed through for inspection of his person, bookbag and anything else coming into the school. Though we realized the detectors weren't an absolute guarantee against weapons, the troopers and school personnel closely oversaw this operation. We considered it essential for self-preservation—and to keep the students from killing one another. The bused students came through the detectors first, followed by the local attendees. No one was allowed to mill around outside or to congregate in the hallways. The action was always more containable when we had everyone dispersed into classrooms.

When the corridors emptied between classes, usually half of the forty or so men assigned to each floor would descend to the cafeteria for coffee and doughnuts and a smoke. By the end of the first week we had it down pat: six class periods and three lunch periods for us to worry about. It was funny—the kids hated classtime, but we loved it. Those were our breaks. While the kids were contained in their classrooms, few fights erupted that couldn't be handled by the flying response squad. We and the kids were together from 7:30 to 1:35 Monday through Friday.

That first week we were all wondering how long this could go on, or at least how long the state force would be involved. And I must have heard this question at least fifty times:

"Hey, Moran—how's it feel to be back in school?"

It was well-known amongst the guys that I'd left the troopers for a while to teach school. I had really enjoyed teaching and interacting with the kids, but after a few years I missed the variety of police work and the idea that I was my own boss. Despite being part of a paramilitary organization with all its attendant strictures, the solitary nature of the work made virtually all the strategic decisions on the job mine alone. After the years spent constantly outdoors in the Berkshires, it was also tough being cooped up in a classroom.

I was a good teacher. Coming back to law enforcement was a tough decision to make. Now look at me, cooped up in school again. The mountain view from my old classroom was certainly different from this. The windows of Southie High looked out over tenement rooftops to the harbor and Dorchester Bay. Gulls sailed past the wire-grilled windows of the school and planed down G Street toward the beach. Many a day on that duty I envied the gulls their freedom.

I think having been a teacher made the duty at Southie even tougher for me than for most of the guys because I could empathize with both sides. I certainly knew it was lousy and dangerous duty for a cop; but I also knew what a terrible toll it exacted from the kids. My idea of education wasn't to spend time trying to keep black kids and white kids from killing each other.

Most of these kids didn't even know why they were fighting half the time; they just felt they were *supposed* to. Some were scared. Some got pumped up with hate at home, while others just followed along, terribly afraid, at that age, of being different from everybody else.

Kids of high school age are confused enough living in their own changing bodies without external stuff like busing and integration to confuse them. Take all those biologic juices, mix in the identity-seeking that goes with that time of life, put the kid in different school surroundings, add a few TV cameras, cops every ten feet and some newspeople who can make you a star at six o'clock if you say or do something provocative enough—what have you got? Certainly not much real education.

Because I'd been a teacher and retained that interest, I spent a lot of time wandering the corridors and listening in the school hallways when the other troopers went for coffee. The two Southie High teachers that I eventually got to know well were both English teachers, as I had been. They were surprised at first by the diversity of my career choices, but delighted to have a sympathetic ear, someone from outside the school system who could share their concerns in this maelstrom.

Slim and attractive, Kathleen O'Donnell had been teaching at Southie for ten years since her graduation from Boston College. She enjoyed teaching in South Boston, helping those she called "her kids." Her kids were those whose parents didn't send them to the private, Jesuit-run Boston College High School or those who couldn't pass the entrance exam to Boston Latin, the city's flagship of academic excellence. The climate had changed at Southie for Kathleen.

Always a problem at the school, discipline was now nonexistent. White teachers had become fearful of sending black students to the office for discipline problems. No matter how strong the justification, they were afraid of being tagged racist. The white administrators held the same fears and self-doubts as the teachers. Black students, like students anywhere, were quick to sense this insecurity and take advantage of it. White students perceived the hesitation of teachers and administrators as racial preference, and they resented it. Returning home each night, they'd report their perception of this preferential treatment, fanning the flames of parental anger even further. Parents then had front-line intelligence to report in the nightly battle of words that accompanied the daily action. Reverse discrimination. *Cui bono?* is a Latin term in law asking who benefits from the situation at hand. In Southie, I couldn't see anyone who was directly benefiting from Judge Garrity's ruling.

Whenever the opportunity arose I would hover in the hallway outside her classroom and watch Kathleen O'Donnell deliver forceful, interesting lectures to her students. The first time I observed her, she was teaching the poetry of Edna St. Vincent Millay. Not the easiest thing in the world, teaching poetry appreciation to kids that age, in these circumstances. I had a hard time with it under normal conditions. With that subject matter I figured her class would erupt into a general brawl after about thirty seconds. What actually happened was that Kathleen's form of control over the kids was so complete that she held them spellbound and taught them poetry. She kept things lively and moving, with questions and interesting points of view. Kathleen let her students know she was in charge at all times, observing that ancient dictum of successful teachers: "He who hesitates is lost."

Watching Kathleen put me in mind of a brash young idealist from the University of Wisconsin who had come to teach at Lee High School in the Berkshires while I was there. Friendly, intelligent and likable, the young midwesterner thought he could get to the kids and teach them with a laid-back style that lacked any particular rules or discipline. He wanted to be buddies with them. He even told his students to call him Ed. Ed didn't last until the Christmas break. The kids ran all over him. I figured he would've lasted about a period and a half at Southie before the kids sent him back to Wisconsin to change his major to animal husbandry.

Despite their conflicting signals and constant threat of rebellion, kids need, and want, some form of control. They don't always like to be told what the guidelines are, but they do need limits. Of course, they are going to be testing those limits at all times. Despite their cries for freedom, they don't want to be in charge. Not always. The busing situation gave them a whole new set of circumstances with no immediately defined limits.

The rules had changed for the teachers too. People like Kathleen O'Donnell had taught kids from these same neighborhoods for years, in pretty much the same way with fairly predictable results. They had a prescribed and acceptable formula for discipline and other problems. In confrontations with students, they had always expected and received (again, within certain realistic limits) support from their school administrators. The frontline teachers had a back-up support system as well: the school department at large, their teachers union and the political structure of the city. Now this was no longer true. They never knew in advance how their reaction to an incident would be taken.

Like the kids, they had their own prejudices and fears. They saw the violent neighborhood reactions to busing; they too had to run a gantlet of citizens who told them they should refuse to teach kids who were bused in. Often they were the targets of auto vandalism

—and kids weren't always the culprits. As each day ended they wondered if they'd make it through another. Easy targets for the media and the students, the teachers had it tough throughout the busing crisis.

The toughest duty for us troopers was the lunch periods. The corridors were bad enough between periods, but the cafeteria was real hell. The three lunch periods per day saw some of the worst violence, almost as if the kids made deals among themselves to defer the real stuff until there was a greater audience.

For one thing the cafeteria was always jammed. It was too small for the number of students at the high school, so there were extra teachers for monitoring and combat-clad troopers jammed against the walls, trying to be unobtrusive. Our orders were to maintain order while trying not to disrupt the educational process— whatever the hell that meant.

Being in that lunchroom a few days as observer was like taking crash courses in adolescent psychology and peer pressure politics. The lunchroom divided down the middle, blacks on one side, whites on the other.

It was incredible to observe how Machiavellian some kids could be, how mature in brinkmanship. Some kids who couldn't add two plus two were extremely capable diplomats. With a few well-chosen taunts or bits of sideline encouragement, they could urge others to risk their lives while never themselves approaching the line of fire. Other kids, not so subtle, just pushed their friends into things they wouldn't chance themselves.

During lunch periods, the tension was incredible. We were always waiting for the next outbreak of violence. After a few days we could sense who were the talkers and who were the doers on each side, so we could at least filter out the extraneous and concentrate on real trouble. The entire first year was like a prolonged staring contest interrupted by frequent outbursts of violence. The blacks would barely touch their food, eyes shifting, on the alert for trouble. The white kids were much the same way. We added a line of troopers at parade rest down the center to keep them apart.

Eventually, the student body was no longer just an amorphous mass of faces. We began to recognize individual students, though we couldn't name them. Some even smiled or nodded occasionally as they passed in the corridors. Some never did.

A few of the kids even tried playing psychological race games with us. Hoping for a reaction, a white kid, say, carrying a tray to the bin, would slow down passing a trooper and smirk, whispering:

"How d'you like babysitting for niggers?"

Black troopers were subjected to the same type of thing, reversed, from black students. To the best of my knowledge and to our professional credit, none of us ever did anything except ignore the remarks, not dignifying them with a response. Some of that race business had worked from September to December, when the Boston PD had been there, because some of the police were from Southie themselves, and de facto segregation was something they wanted to defend, not eliminate. Everyone brings his own prejudices to his work. Of course it was in our interest to maintain a professional and objective distance from the students.

We would've liked more distance from some kids. In many ways, Red was the archetypal problem student at Southie. Trouble followed Red like night follows day. His appearance on any scene was usually the signal for all hell to break loose. Small-built, but wiry and quick, Red was a product of the Southie housing projects and rated by us observers as the best and one of the most prolific fighters in the school. His archrival among the blacks was a kid named Reynold. From Roxbury, Reynold was bigger than Red and no slouch with his fists. Whenever these two had something going between them, and that was most days, it was like High Noon in the corridors. There was no way we could keep up with everything. Only quick action by several teachers and troopers headed off a number of serious altercations between the two. Red gave the impression of being slow-witted, but I always felt he was about four steps ahead of us adults. An incident that happened the following school year proved he was certainly a step or two ahead of me at least.

As we muddled into spring, I wondered if summer would ever come again, allowing us to get out of South Boston and the tension for a while. Extra duty in the busing situation eventually evolved into overtime. A trooper could accept or refuse any extra hours, which were an opportunity for many to make some heavy money. When it became voluntary, I refused it because I was in my last year of grad school and the strain of the school and the normal demands of the job, not to mention the busing situation, were already unraveling my marriage. A high divorce rate is a sad commentary on police work, but it has become a given. That doesn't make it any more enjoyable.

In the beginning, double time shifts were mandatory. We were being paid for travel time, but who wanted to commute a hundred miles each way, especially after a shift of combat duty in Southie High? At that time we couldn't bunk in the academy because a class was in their training cycle, so many of us rented motel rooms around the Framingham area, outside Boston.

Finally, the school year ended. We returned to our regular assignments, but it was obvious from the nightly news bulletins that we'd be back to Southie in the fall. As bad as things had seemed that first year, it was beginning to look like things could be worse. During the previous year the size of the force held in reserve in case of emergency was reduced—now rumor had it the overall number of troopers in the schools would also be reduced. The Hart-Dean Annex was closing. Major personnel shifts were proposed and Dr. Reid, the long-term incumbent, was about to be replaced as headmaster at Southie High.

Released from Southie for the summer, I was returned to the Berkshire mountains and reassigned as court prosecutor out of the Pittsfield barracks. The court wasn't at full tilt during the summer, and it was the type of duty I needed to recover from the constant tension of integretion duty.

Almost daily, I'd be in my car by 3:30, following my nose to the smell of greens clippings and pine cones. The nearest golf course served as my therapy couch for the day as I worked out all the pent-up tension and frustration chasing that little white golf ball down the fairways. I've played nowhere else in the world that has trees so dense and pervasive as the forests bordering the golf courses of the Berkshires. That summer I played every day, until darkness drove me off the course.

I played a lot of golf that summer because I was tired of trying to explain the situation in South Boston to people in the Berkshires, people who had their own preconceived notions of the truth anyway. In the past I'd often gotten some nice ego gratification from friends and neighbors who assumed that as a trooper I always had the inside scoop on public events, and who listened to my opinions as if they carried some weight. This time the frustration far outweighed the satisfaction.

As the glory of August waned I felt the bittersweet regret that every kid in the civilized world has felt, knowing the freedom of summer was coming to an end. Over the summer, nothing in the political scene had changed to keep us from returning to Southie as we'd all hoped. First day of school we rolled out of the mountains and back to the heights.

This year our unit massed at the Commonwealth Pier, leaving our cruisers there instead of out at Framingham. I no longer had to lead a convoy of strangers. We assembled at 0600, then bused to our duty locations. I was back at the high school.

The exterior of the building hadn't changed, but there was a world of difference inside. The old guard of staff and administration was gone. A new broom had swept clean. Along with the headmaster, Reid, gone also were Kathleen O'Donnell and school old-timers like Joe Crowley, the coach and athletic director who'd led Southie to so many city championships. The old staff was replaced by a crowd of younger, eager and, though less experienced, no less enthusiastic teachers and administrators. The new group was obviously chosen for racial representation, with a heavy flavoring of minorities. In addition, a corps of guidance counselors and school psychologists was now part of the staff. A disused area behind the school auditorium had been renovated and a series of cubicles erected for the new staff to function in. Money was pouring in from somewhere.

The biggest change had been the replacement of Dr. Reid, the affable headmaster, a good man in the wrong place at the wrong time. Even if he'd been on the verge of solving the situation, he probably would've been replaced so it would look to the public like the politicians were doing something. And firing the boss is usually good for action credits. Hiring someone new from far away also makes it look like the politicans worked hard at finding a replacement. Sometimes they simply pick the applicant from the farthest distance away—or the one from a city it was fun to take junkets to.

Jerome Winegar was named new headmaster. Winegar received great press from the *Globe,* which wrote glowing reports of the job he'd done implementing integration measures as a principal in the

Minneapolis-St. Paul school system. A large, friendly bear of a man, Winegar exuded an air of enthusiasm for this distasteful task and seemed eager to succeed. He was constantly roaming the hallways, making himself visible to the staff and students.

The antibusing forces picketing outside the school had some colorful and graphic suggestions for where they wished Winegar to draw his next assignment. I called the protesters rednecks because of their negative attitude toward accepting the desegregation of their schools, but I often wonder how I might have reacted if I'd awoken to find an invasion force camped on my doorstep.

Later on during busing duty I had some disagreement with Winegar over the way he handled his assignment. Southie High originally had about eighteen hundred kids enrolled. This number dropped radically after busing started, but Winegar was still releasing daily totals stating an enrollment somewhere around nine hundred. The troopers took a head count that showed these figures to be greatly inflated. I took issue with Winegar until I realized he was doing what he thought best to defuse the situation. By shifting kids into various programs throughout the city, he avoided a more violent confrontation than he already had on his hands.

The troopers assigned to the new, flimsily constructed counseling area behind the auditorium couldn't help but overhear and got quite an earful during the early weeks of school. The timid new counselors, many of them barely older than the students, were using the buddy-up approach to attempt to solve the behavior problems of the unruly students sent to them. Again, kids test the limits. Immediately sensing the inexperience and softline well-meaning of the new people, the kids played them like experts, displaying the most outrageous conduct and using language with the new teachers and counselors that went beyond even what was previously bizarre for Southie.

This situation presented a problem for troopers who had seen the effectiveness of the previous year's methods in dealing with troublemakers. Now we were seeing the new counselors pleading with kids to behave, rather than ordering them to. You can guess what this did for general discipline in the school. In the face of mounting problems, this new permissiveness was particularly frustrating for us because he had to put a lid on the problems that the new attitude was exacerbating.

On the second floor I met and observed Kathleen O'Donnell's replacement. John was young, fat and friendly. He reminded me of somebody's family pet. John could relate to other teachers and us troopers, but he had serious problems in the classroom. After observing a few periods, it was obvious to me that he'd never make it. John should have chosen a different profession. He had two strikes against him. Firstly, he lacked experience and force of personality. He never established a position of leadership and control in the classroom. Secondly, he really had no grasp of the subject matter he wanted to teach. The kids might not know the subject matter either, but they can spot a bullshitter from a hundred yards away. The result was mayhem, anarchy. The kids simply ignored him. They talked openly about anything they wanted to and roamed the classroom at will.

I believe John was put into this untenable situation simply because he was a minority. He was not qualified. As a result, he suffered as much as the kids assigned to classes under him. I believe this new pattern of hiring was a harmful by-product of busing. The parent activist groups wanted more black teachers in the system—they got them. Teaching qualifications weren't the issue; skin color was. Throughout the crisis, political considerations outweighed sound educational policy. Granted, something had to be done to accomplish wider integration. But everyone would have been better served if, instead of trying to obtain instant racial balance among the faculty and students, the court had insisted that the highest quality teachers be assigned to Southie and other schools deemed to have been giving lower quality education. That step certainly would have lowered the level of disruption and violence. People like John were just thrown in like cannon fodder. Kathleen O'Donnell's replacement was as much a victim as the students, black or white.

At night it was great entertainment for those of us intimately involved with the situation to pick up *The Boston Globe* and read the stories penned by Muriel Cohen, an education writer. Muriel wrote about the war zone conditions at Southie High as if they were some kind of marvellous, innovative educational experiment. For the most part, her stuff was so far from reality that we questioned whether she'd even visited the site. To back up her own statements she'd quote grossly inflated daily attendance figures.

They jibed with what the city administration wanted everyone to believe, but they were patently false to anyone on the scene. Kindness leads me to conclude she reported what she saw through rose-colored glasses. What she reported as a marvellous educational experience, I saw as a macabre horror show that would traumatize an entire generation of students.

Regardless of its history-making impact on the city and Commonwealth, and the cliff-edge excitement of imminent violence, integration duty at Southie High was ultimately reduced to routine. Boring routine.

For those of us with inside duty, the response squad was a chance to break the routine of corridor and lunchroom duty. The response squad was a reserve force held ready to counter outbreaks anywhere in the school. At times kids tried to assert themselves by taking over a classroom or holding a hostage. It meant a heavy physical workout up and down the stairs, in and out of the various classrooms the squad might be called to in an emergency. I'd been frequently assigned and enjoyed the freedom and diversity of roaming around and being in all the action.

This day I was in command of the response squad for the first time. Newly promoted to corporal, I was eager to impress. I headquartered the squad in the first floor hallway, from where we'd respond swiftly to whatever floor our trouble calls came from. We were busy that day, running from one end of the school to the other, up and down the staircases, covering flare-ups of trouble. Most of it was due to an outbreak of spring fever, but there were some lingering disagreements from a general riot the previous day.

Our last call had been a false alarm all the way up to the fourth floor. Again. Trooper Al Rivet signaled he was out of breath. I ordered a rest break before returning to our station on the first floor.

"Take five," I said, gasping myself, as I slumped down to rest against the wall. "That must be the tenth time today we've flown up those stairs."

The squad followed my example, slouching to the floor and easing off their clumsy helmets.

Al Rivet crossed his legs. "Hey, Corporal, one question," he said, slowly regaining his breath. "Why don't we stay up here on the fourth floor and respond downward? Can't we run downstairs when we're called, instead of up every time?"

The other troopers in the squad shook sweat droplets to the floor, nodding their vehement approval of Al's brilliant idea.

I felt like a jerk. The leader. Why hadn't I thought of it first, instead of having us kill ourselves hammering up the stairs every time? The one thing I didn't want to do when promoted was make some of the same kind of dumb mistakes I'd been made to suffer under by shortsighted leaders. I guessed these guys would just figure me a little dense. Just another dumb corporal, I could hear them thinking.

"Good idea, Al," I admitted.

"Wasn't mine," Al said. That was some compensation, at least.

"Too smart for headquarters," I said. "Whose idea was it, then?"

"You know Red, that *slow* kid we're always having the jams with in the lunchroom?" Rivet asked.

I nodded, knowing before Rivet confirmed it that Red was going to outdo me in the brain department.

"Yesterday, when you weren't here, Red saw us all panting like this after running upstairs," Rivet said. "He's the one. Red suggested us old guys'd be better off responding down from the fourth, rather than up from the first." Just what I needed to hear. Red makes a command decision for me. Like any great idea, it seemed obvious after it was revealed.

And they said these kids weren't learning anything?

Just then the bell rang and the kids poured into the hallway for class change. The students at Southie High that morning must have wondered why the response squad was rolling around on the floor, laughing. Their hotshot new corporal had been outthought by a juvenile delinquent.

15. Shootout: Quick Action

I wish they all went down this way...

Time: Recent
Location: East Boston
Duty: Airport

The only truly consistent rule of police work is that you can always expect the unexpected. And, like a blue application of Murphy's Law, when the unexpected happens, it happens at the wrong time with everyone in the wrong place.

I was relaxing over a morning mug at the US Air coffee shop when the two ex-cons stuck guns in young Susan Keohane's pretty face. Susan worked at the Exxon gas station on the main thoroughfare at Logan Airport. Home on a semester break, Susan was helping her father, Joe, who managed the station.

While I was sipping coffee, Joe Keohane was out at the islands pumping gas while his daughter worked the register inside the office. Looking up from counting the bills in her register, Susan found herself at eye level with the barrels of "two huge-looking guns."

"They started waving those cannons around, making a lot of crazy threats about what they'd do if anything happened, or they didn't get what they wanted. They could take *anything* they wanted and I'd help them carry it out to their car, long as they didn't shoot," Susan said later.

The two bandits reached into the open cash drawer and scooped out a thousand dollars in bills that Susan had just finished counting. They seemed satisfied. Backing out, they jumped into their waiting car and sped out the back service road that led to the air-port cargo area and an employee exit.

Alerted by Susan, Joe Keohane grabbed the phone. Somehow managing to remain calm, he dialed the Troop F station number. The state police station house is located in the terminal area within a few hundred yards of Keohane's business. Within seconds a description of the car and its occupants was broadcast to all state police cruisers in the area, plus the Boston police net.

Minutes later Corporal Jim Harrington spotted the robbery car in Day Square, East Boston. He broadcast his location to head-quarters and began following the fleeing robbers.

Two Troop F detectives, Sergeant Carmen Tammaro and Trooper Dick Davis, were on their way to East Boston Court. Hearing Harrington's radio transmission, they wheeled around and headed for Day Square.

When the call reporting the armed robbery and giving a descrip-tion of the getaway car came to them, Trooper Twomey and Sergeant Windisch had their hands full of papers. They were on the outbound side of the airport road, citing a Boston cab for numerous traffic and safety violations. Then they got the call, "Trooper in pursuit."

Throwing the vehicle papers back at the cabbie, they headed out of the airport, lights flashing and siren screaming, to help fellow trooper Harrington. Their cruiser practically flew—until they got to the artery that connects the airport with East Boston and other communities. Rush hour was in full bloom.

The two fugitives had been slowed by traffic as well. Unable to make an unimpeded bolt for freedom, they got the jitters. When they saw Harrington's cruiser tailing them, they figured it was too quick to be a response to the holdup. It had to be coincidence; especially since this cruiser displayed no lights or sirens. Not want-ing to appear conspicuous or do anything to top off a cruiser that wasn't after them, the escapees struggled not to run for it. They maintained an even pace in traffic. Which they managed until the two other cruisers bansheed in behind Harrington.

Now things picked up. The nondescript station wagon piloted by the fugitives accelerated to top speed. Careening through East Boston's Italian neighborhoods, the car zigzagged wildly, carom-ing off cars parked on either side of the narrow streets. The three cruisers followed behind like the tail of a snake.

Windisch and Twomey tried to pass Corporal Harrington's slower cruiser on East Boston's logjammed streets. They started around, getting almost parallel when an oncoming truck forced them back in between Harrington and the fugitives. They held there.

Now the detectives in the other car, Tammaro and Davis, saw their chance. On Condor, they swung out on the wider street and gunned it, pulling alongside the escaping vehicle. They shouted orders at the wagon to pull over.

Windisch and Twomey, now directly behind the action, saw the passenger in the escape vehicle level a weapon at Tammaro and Davis in the detective's car. Dan Twomey responded quickly from behind, thrusting his revolver out the side window of the rocketing cruiser and throwing a round at the wagon.

The back window of the getaway vehicle exploded from the magnum round. The man who had been about to shoot at the detectives now turned, firing rounds back at Windisch and Twomey.

Nearing Meridian Street, the station wagon slowed. The passenger's door opened. The man doing all the shooting burst out of the wagon, landing in a roll. He jumped to his feet and scooted away between some tightly packed three-family houses.

The wagon had sped off before the man hit the ground. Detectives Tammaro and Davis screeched their car to a halt and pursued the gunman on foot. The other two cruisers continued chasing after the station wagon.

With the troopers in hot pursuit, the driver of the escape wagon raced off, heading for the Chelsea bridge. Out of heavy traffic now, he picked up yet more speed. He didn't even slow for the red light near the bridge, bashing off a car that was legitimately crossing the intersection. As his cruiser roared past in hot pursuit of the wagon, Twomey noted the shocked glare of the innocent driver sitting at the wheel of his suddenly immobilized sedan.

At the other phase of the chase, breathing hard from the lengthy foot chase, the detectives were having a difficult time tracking their husky young suspect through the confusing maze of back yards on Falcon Street. They were about ready to halt for an oxygen break when Sergeant Tammaro suddenly spied their quarry scrambling up a fence in the next yard.

Tammaro ordered, "Halt," then squeezed off a shot.

The suspect disappeared over the fence.

Davis and Tammaro climbed over after him. Gone. That yard was empty and there was no trace of him all the way back out to Falcon Street. They'd lost their man.

Back-up cruisers, including my own, were now arriving to assist. I joined forces with Trooper Dick Davis. An angry Tammaro went to the radio to broadcast a more detailed description of the suspect: six feet, two hundred pounds, later twenties; wearing blue jeans and a red, yellow and blue woolen shirt. Probably armed.

The back-up forces dispersed to help search the area.

Meanwhile, Windisch and Twomey were furious at themselves for also having lost sight of their quarry. The wagon had rolled around several corners in succession, eluding the troopers.

But only momentarily: Windisch spotted it again on Congress, racing toward the end of the street. The troopers pursued as the wagon cut down a side street. Only split-seconds behind as they turned the corner onto Walnut, they came upon the suspect's battered and smoking vehicle, stopped in front of some abandoned apartment houses. Empty. Not a soul in sight.

The rear window was blown out, the car's sides were a mass of scrapes and dents from collisions, and the front was accordioned from the crash at the intersection. There were a number of spent cartridge casings scattered on the seat and floor. A search of the immediate area yielded nothing. They called for a K-9 unit to assist and reported the license number of the demolished getaway vehicle.

The registration check listed the vehicle owner as Angela Ullven of Sagamore Avenue, Chelsea. The car was towed to the airport barracks area where it was immediately gone over by state police print men, chemists and ballistics experts.

While this was going on, Troopers O'Malley and Flaherty of the Major Crimes Unit spoke with Chief Charlie Wilson and his cooperative detectives from the Chelsea department. They were told that Donald Ullven, son of the listed owner of the escape vehicle, had a criminal record a mile long and that the Peabody police on the North Shore had a current photo of him. A call to Peabody elicited their swift help. They sent a pair of their detectives to the airport with the Ullven photo, hoping it could be identified by the station owner, Joe Keohane.

The photo from Peabody was mixed with several other mug shots to make the choice as objective as possible. Keohane gave identification immediately, pulling the Peabody police photo from the crowd. The troopers exulted. Donald Ullven was positively identified as one of their fugitives.

Back at the scene of the failed foot chase, Trooper Davis and I were still searching the area where the first gunman had escaped after rolling out of the car. We were concentrating our search on the ground between the houses on Falcon Street where the suspect had scrambled over the fence after being shot at, eluding Davis and Tammaro. Finally—eureka!

There was great joy in Mudville when our microscopic search turned up a .380 semiautomatic pistol. We rushed the weapon to the ballistics people for a comparison test against the spent cartridges. Dick Davis was then dispatched to East Boston District Court to obtain an armed robbery warrant for the arrest of Donald Ullven. The pieces were starting to come together.

At five p.m., an informant phoned Troop F detective Andy Palombo. Palombo was told Ullven had been seen near the Lynnway Motel on Route 1A in the city of Lynn. Bingo. Detective Palombo and I were detailed, along with Troopers Powers, Saltzman and Higginbotham, to proceed to the motel and apprehend Ullven.

At the scene, Powers and Higginbotham were assigned outside surveillance of the motel units while the plainclothes officers, Saltzman, Palombo and I, entered the Italian restaurant connected with the motel. From the foyer, we identified a man seated in the bar as Donald Ullven, using the photo that had been circulated.

In the hope of remaining unnoticed until we got as close as possible, the three of us split up, entering the lounge from separate directions. Donald Ullven sat at the bar, calmly conversing with the barmaid. He appeared too serene to be a fugitive from arrest who'd earlier ditched a getaway car in East Boston after exchanging gunfire with the State Police. But we weren't taking any chances.

My gun held out of sight along my leg, I strolled up to the bar behind Ullven, as if I were going to order a drink.

"State Police," I barked from Ullven's rear, raising the weapon. "Hands in sight, turn around—very slowly!"

Ullven did as ordered, slowly swivelling to face three .357 magnums. He surrendered without a struggle.

From Ullven we took the key to room number sixteen in the motel. We quickly surrounded and searched the room, but Ullven's accomplice had either flown already or never been there. We took Ullven to his room for interrogation.

As they were directly involved in Ullven's pursuit, Windisch and Twomey were summoned and given the privilege of questioning the suspect. Ullven now so shaky he looked like he'd fall apart. We assumed Ullven's fear was motivated by the sight of so many officers with guns or the knowledge that he was righteously nailed. But it soon became clear he was primarily afraid of his partner-in-crime. Ullven agreed to talk, but only if he were protected and taken away from the motel, where his accomplice might show. He was convinced his partner would kill him for cooperating. He wouldn't name him until he felt safe.

Leaving a detail in hiding in case the accomplice returned, we agreed to Ullven's terms, taking him back to F Troop headquarters at the airport. It was 8:30 when we obtained from Donald Ullven the name of his accomplice, William "Billy C" Ceria. Ullven reported that Ceria, a Salem resident, was a parolee from Walpole State Prison.

This information backed up investigative work just completed by other troopers. While Ullven was being questioned, the telephone company had traced phone numbers found in his possession. Two of those numbers went to different floors of the same address in Salem, 30 Symonds Street. The second-floor phone at 30 Symonds was listed to William R. Ceria.

State prison officials at Walpole advised troopers that Boston police had recent photos of Ceria. A trooper was immediately sent to the BPD for a copy that was then rushed back for the official legal identification by Ullven.

"That's Billy C," he said. Ceria's mug shot was photocopied and passed out to all the troopers. Ullven repeatedly stressed strong doubt that Ceria would ever allow himself to be taken alive.

Joseph Faretra, Clerk of the East Boston District Court, immediately issued arrest warrants for Ceria, as well as search warrants for the first and second floors of the house in Salem. It was after midnight, but nobody complained about the hours they were working.

By two in the morning we had the Ceria house surrounded. Hoping for surprise, we approached in silence. Surprise was important, both for succeeding at our mission and increasing the odds of us coming out unhurt; but overriding both was the consideration that there might be children on either floor of the two-family house. The first floor was now known to belong to Ceria's sister. We'd learned she had a young family. Everything we'd heard pointed to Billy C coming out shooting. Anyone who had dealt with Billy C attested to his penchant for violence.

In that dark neighborhood street I recalled the stark fear that our first fugitive, Ullven, had of Ceria, his own partner. Ceria's promise not to be taken alive sounded very plausible for his criminal profile. Ullven had said that Ceria was forever repeating a vow: "No way they'll get me back to prison without shooting me first..." We had to go on the assumption he meant it.

Our plan had to include the possibility of children present. We had to eliminate or disable Ceria as quickly as possible. I called the assault teams together.

"Look, we're just short of 100 percent certain Ceria's in there. Whatever happens, we have to be careful of bystanders. Once we're in final position, troopers from the Peabody barracks will simultaneously dial the numbers for both floors of the house," I said. "Whoever answers from the house will be told to switch on the lights. Then they'll be given one minute to come out, unharmed. That should at least give us the tip-off which floor Billy C is on."

We got into position. Windisch, Foley and I were armed with shotguns. We would assault the first floor, if necessary. Palombo, Dan Twomey and Red McDonald were poised to hit the second floor. Other troopers covered possible escape routes in back and on the side.

At the signal, the simultaneous calls were made to the numbers in the dwelling. No response on the first floor. Second floor, a male voice answered, hung up. We thought it was Ceria. The command was given: "GO!"

Smashing through the outer door, we poured into the darkened first floor of the house. The others pounded up the stairs to the second floor. Foley and Windisch swung the barrels of their shotguns, following in the wake of the beam from my powerful light.

Behind us we heard the sound of bare feet coming across the floor.

I jerked the light around—into the blinking eyes of two half-asleep ten-year-olds. Three other children were found still asleep in their beds. No gun-wielding Ceria.

Upstairs, where the male voice had answered the phone, a woman identifying herself as Ceria's sister told the officers that the children downstairs belonged to her, except for a neighbor's kid who was sleeping over. No she hadn't seen her brother...Billy? No, not in several weeks.

Rummaging around the apartment, Andy Palombo came across $980 in tens and twenties, stuffed into a sugar bowl.

"Just twenty dollars shy of what was stolen from the airport Exxon," Palombo said.

"Quite a coincidence." But no, Ceria's sister didn't know how the money got there. Yes, she was sure—it was weeks since she'd seen her brother.

While Palombo was questioning her about the money, Twomey and Jack O'Malley found some backstairs and followed them to a third-floor sleeping area, a converted attic with two rooms. The beds had been slept in. Yanking the bed aside in one room they found a hole in the wall leading to a crawl-way. Twomey scrunched in with his light. Nothing on the right. Moving left, Twomey spotted two feet and prison-style dungaree bottoms. Backing out quickly, he alerted his partners.

Our team rushed upstairs to assist. Now tearfully admitting her brother was hiding in the crawl-way, the sister swore on her children's lives that Ceria was unarmed.

"He dropped his gun, going over a fence in Eastie."

She insisted that was Billy C's only weapon. Ceria refused orders to come out. He didn't shoot, either. He'd have to shoot through the walls to get at us at this point, but that was a pretty good indication he was indeed unarmed. We weren't too inclined to take the sister's word without some kind of corroboration.

After repeating the exit order several times, we smashed through the sheetrock and pulled him out. Ceria was cuffed, dragged out of the house, and taken to the Peabody barracks.

At 9:30 a.m., Donald Ullven and William Ceria were arraigned before Judge Ferrino in East Boston for armed robbery and assault with intent to murder. The judge entered pleas of not guilty for them and ordered them held in one hundred thousand dollar cash bail.

It was exactly twenty-four hours after the robbery had taken place. The felons were charged and behind bars. Most important, no one had been injured. The case was a model of cooperation between jurisdictions, involving several municipalities and several areas of authority and expertise.

Professional cooperation had allowed the troopers to identify the felons, track them down and apprehend them—all in several different locations. Despite the almost constant peril to themselves and the continuous presence of innocent bystanders, including children, the operation was accomplished without harm to the public.

All the airport troopers involved in the incident, Palombo, Davis and Twomey, Tammaro and Foley, Windisch and I, made civilian safety our overriding concern during the case, not the danger to ourselves. Given Billy C's promise of a shootout, we had to take every precaution—even if it meant additional peril to ourselves—to ensure that no innocent bystander, especially the children, be hurt. Proudly, I can say that that attitude is typical of the men who serve as troopers.

16. Missing

She just believed no one would ever hurt her.

Time: 1981
Location: Airport
Duty: Missing persons search

Located at the base of the massive control tower, the Troop F station office at Logan Airport sits between Terminals B and C, snuggled next to the medical station and, either prophetically or accidentally, Our Lady of the Airways Catholic Chapel.

In addition to visits from regular attendees like Sergeant Carmen Tammaro, a lot of praying goes on at the Logan Airport Chapel. Logan has seven thousand employees of its own, and nearly forty million people pass through the airport each year. The church has the distinction of being the first airport chapel in the country, opened in 1952 under the charismatic leadership of the late Cardinal Cushing. A forward thinker, Cushing said the church should go where the people were. He must have sensed the future of air travel.

Our Lady's present pastor, Father Bernard McLaughlin, says the state troopers are some of the chapel's steadiest customers. Sergeant Tammaro rarely misses Sunday Mass there, but trooper Arthur "Red" MacDonald went him one better, marrying his fiancee, Patricia, in the chapel in 1980. Father McLaughlin also christened their daughter Shannon, and son Casey, in the airport church.

Until the Sunday after Thanksgiving Day, 1981, not one of those forty million people passing through had ever been lost. Not completely. Not permanently. Until the mysterious disappearance of Joan Webster.

Petite, attractive, Harvard graduate student Joan Webster disappeared from Logan Airport after returning from a Thanksgiving holiday visit with her parents in New Jersey. She simply vanished. Last seen alive at the Eastern Airlines terminal November 28, 1981. The resulting years-long search for Joan Webster included many state agencies and police forces. I helped raise sunken boats and scour the murky floor of Boston Harbor as police tried to close in on suspected murderer Leonard "Lenny the Quahog" Paradiso.

The Sunday after Thanksgiving is a day most F Troopers would rather not have to work because it's one of the heaviest air traffic volume days. Cars attempting to get in and out of the airport by the short access roads through the Sumner and Callahan tunnels cause heavy gridlock.

When Joan Webster failed to turn up at Harvard long after her expected arrival time, her anxious roommates contacted her parents in New Jersey. The attempt to locate her began. Sergeant Tammaro was the duty detective who received the missing persons report on Joan Webster. State police detectives were called in because, although no one lives at Logan Airport and therefore cannot technically be reported missing from there, the Eastern terminal was the last place the Webster girl had been seen.

The missing girl's parents arrived with police from the Harvard University force. Tammaro listened patiently to Terry and George Webster. He noted the patrician manner of the Ivy Leaguer's parents, particularly Mr. Webster, whose coolness suggested a lot of experience with crisis. Webster was Yankee Brahmin handsome, reminding the detective of a John Singer Sargent portrait. His very manner bespoke authority, as though he was used to having his orders obeyed. Early on, he was pegged as a federal bureaucrat, though his occupation listing was otherwise.

This early in the investigation, Tammaro wasn't overly concerned. Carmen had heard countless similar stories of disappearances, especially of young people, in the years he'd been assigned to the airport. Almost invariably the parents or spouse suspected kidnapping, and in almost every case the missing person turned up later, fine. Sometimes it was simply a misunderstanding of arrival dates or times; sometimes it was a relationship gone sour or job pressure or failing grades at school that caused people to "disappear" for a while.

Tammaro told the Websters he believed there probably was a valid, though yet to be understood, reason for their daughter's absence.

"Nonetheless," he assured them, "we'll be doing everything in our power to locate your girl."

The parents left, relieved by Sergeant Tammaro's efficient manner and constant smile.

Tammaro assigned Detective John "J.J." Kelly to assist the university police in their investigation. Kelly escorted the Harvard investigator to the Eastern Airlines area where they viewed the passenger manifests and questioned anyone who could possibly have seen Joan Webster that night. Flight attendants, baggage handlers and other ground personnel were all shown photos of the Webster girl. The processed ticket coupon/boarding pass was located in Miami, Eastern's HQ. That record verified that Joan had indeed deplaned at Boston. With witness testimony, the detectives were able to trace Joan to the point where she was seen picking up her luggage after leaving the aircraft. Then her trail simply vanished.

Beginning the next day, the media daily requested information on the whereabouts of the attractive grad student. Nothing turned up; nor did Joan herself show up to prove Tammaro's theory. When nothing happened for several weeks, public interest flagged.

Then the story bounced back into the headlines. Joan's purse and wallet were recovered in a salt marsh in Saugus, Massachusetts off the Lynn-Revere marsh road, Route 107. At that point the Saugus police also assigned a detective to assist the Harvard University police in the investigation. At this juncture, Harvard still had the primary jurisdiction in the case—technically, Joan had disappeared from the university.

No new developments followed the discovery of the purse and wallet. At least nothing solid. Months passed. In January, one of Joan's suitcases was found in a locker in the Greyhound terminal in Park Square, downtown Boston. At roughly the same time, Suffolk County District Attorney Newman Flanagan assigned Timothy Burke, one of his young assistant D.A.'s to supervise the reinvestigation of several unresolved murder cases, cases that for various reasons had never been brought to trial.

Quiet, softspoken Tim Burke was not the typical brash assistant D.A. A transplant from upstate New York, he'd been quietly building a reputation as a very able, aggressive and successful prosecutor in Newman Flanagan's office. One of the most intriguing cases in the dossier handed Burke was the Marie Ianuzzi murder. Young Marie Ianuzzi's strangled body had been found in August 1979 behind a vacant lobster pound on the Lynn marsh road in Saugus.

Though Burke was not yet aware of the startling similarities between the Webster disappearance and the Ianuzzi murder, one event had already occurred that would later figure heavily in the Webster case. Pretty Marie Ianuzzi's corpse had been discovered in *the same marshy area*, a scant few hundred feet from where the purse and wallet of Joan Webster had been found shortly after her disappearance.

After Joan's luggage turned up, the Webster parents requested a meeting of all official parties concerned with their daughter's disappearance. Present at Harvard in late February were representatives from three different county district attorney's offices, as well as a state police officer from each office and the Logan Airport detective unit. Lieutenant Colonel John R. O'Donovan, chief of all state police detectives, attended, in addition to the people from the Harvard and Saugus departments.

This full house agreed that Tim Burke should supervise the Webster case with the help of Troop F detective Andrew Palombo. It was generally conceded by those who knew both men that they'd leave no stone unturned in their zealous handling of the Webster investigation.

Just prior to the meeting, D.A. Tim Burke had sought out airport detective Palombo for his help regarding the then two-year-old Marie Ianuzzi murder case. Burke had heard through the police grapevine that Andy Palombo was the one cop that knew the most details regarding the case. Much of big Andy's knowledge of the case and the people involved came from his extensive undercover work around East Boston. Burke and Palombo would make an extremely effective team.

Before his marriage to Christine and the taming influence of fatherhood, Andy's passion had been speed—fast cars and motorcycles, though he'd flown airplanes as well. He loved to buy classic Jags and Corvettes and rebuild them for resale. An associate once said Andy had more cars than a Saudi prince.

At six-foot-four and 230 pounds, Andrew C. Palombo looked every bit the defensive lineman he'd been in college before joining the troopers. Andy was a forceful questioner. It was difficult to ignore him. But it was his easygoing manner that made him so good undercover. People tended to confide in him. D.A. Burke found Andy to be a storehouse of information about the airport and the East Boston community surrounding it. Because he was scrupulously honest, fair and efficient, Andy Palombo had a veritable bank of informants.

Detective Palombo began the arduous task of interviewing the family, friends and classmates of the missing Joan Webster, work that had all been carefully done before; but there is always hope of turning up something new.

He wasn't long into the marathon of interviewing witnesses and studying personal articles and pictures of the Webster girl before Andy felt he knew her. It didn't help. There was nothing to suggest Joan Webster dropped out of sight of her own volition. Neither his own intuition, the comments of parents nor the insights and guesses of friends gave Palombo any logical reason to assume Joan Webster ran away. Andy knew that this was not simply another case of a poor little rich girl opting out of society by running off with a boyfriend or rebelling from parental authority. Andy was quickly convinced Joan Webster had been a victim of foul play.

How many times did Andy read the description on the *Missing* poster? The photo showed a smiling, comely girl. Height five-foot-three, weight 112 pounds. Joan's long, dark brown hair hung straight from a center part and matched her dark eyes.

Andy learned that clean-cut, preppie-looking Joan Webster had majored in art and design as an undergraduate. She'd landed a good job with a prestigious New York design company and after two years of hard work had gained a considerable reputation in the firm for her design work. Feeling she'd eventually be even more successful if she earned her masters, she applied for the two-year MFA program at Harvard's Graduate School of Design. She was halfway through her first year when she disappeared from Logan.

Palombo could recite the poster blurb from memory: "Last seen at Boston Logan Airport at the Eastern Airlines terminal on Saturday evening, November 28, 1981, wearing long, brown, chesterfield-style coat, black worsted suit, red print blouse. Carrying large, tan, suede tote bag containing phonograph records, architectural pamphlets, etc.'' The clear brown eyes staring from the photo looked so trusting...Andy thought of his own four young girls.

Twenty-year-old Marie Ianuzzi had long dark hair as well. Though hitting the wall in the Webster case, Detective Palombo and D.A. Burke were making exciting headway in the Ianuzzi murder. They'd dredged up new evidence pointing in the direction of Lenny the Quahog.

Marie Ianuzzi and her boyfriend had been guests at a wedding reception when another of the invited guests started paying an inordinate amount of attention to her. That other guest was Lenny the Quahog, a husky parolee from Walpole State Prison. Lenny was out after serving time for assault with attempt to rape. Police had caught him choking a hitchhiker in a roadside rest area. Paradiso had a long history of sexual assaults, and as of 1986 he is awaiting trial for charges of assault with intent to rape and murder another hitchhiker near his girlfriend's Revere home in 1980. After some initial hassle at the wedding party, including an argument between Marie Ianuzzi and her boyfriend, she left the party with Lenny The Quahog. Her body was found behind the vacant lobster pound on the Lynn tidal marshes on August 12. Marie Ianuzzi had been strangled.

Leonard Paradiso had earned his nickname by selling clams and quahogs at the ethnic feasts in Boston's Italian North End. Paradiso was a local occasional shellfisherman who also sometimes ran a shellfish business in Bangor, Maine. He also had a boat; a 26-foot Chris-craft cruiser called the Malafemmena, from which he'd tried his hand at other types of fishing as well as lobstering.

During questioning Paradiso was asked the whereabouts of his car so that it could be searched. A witness had testified to seeing a car, matching the description of Lenny's, stopped on the Lynn marsh road the night Marie was killed. Paradiso claimed it had been stolen after he'd dropped off the woman. He said he'd been home with his girlfriend at the time she was allegedly murdered. Lenny the Quahog was returned to prison for parole violation.

While working on the Ianuzzi case, Andy Palombo received a call from a reliable informant who "wanted to talk about Lenny Paradiso."

"The Quahog?" Andy said, perking up. He expected a fresh lead on the Ianuzzi case but was experienced enough to leave his question open-ended. "What about the Quahog?"

"That Harvard kid, Webster."

Palombo flashed Tim Burke immediately.

"Joan Webster?" Andy fought to slow his breathing. "You have information on Joan Webster?"

"She's dead."

The informant presented a scenario of the night of the alleged murder. He told them that Lenny, well-dressed and presentably groomed, struck up a conversation with the young woman while standing in the cab line at the Eastern terminal. When Webster innocently mentioned that she was traveling to Cambridge, Paradiso told young Joan that he too lived in Cambridge and would be delighted to give her a ride. Supposedly, Joan accepted.

During the four years Andy Palombo worked on the Webster case, he faced a recurrent and nagging question—why would a young woman bright enough to be a grad student at Harvard accept a ride from a total stranger at an airport? Especially a stranger at the unexalted level of social graces attained by Lenny the Quahog? Burke and Palombo spent many sessions trading opinions about her willingness to go. After countless hours of interviews with family and close friends, Palombo eventually concluded that despite her professional achievements, Joan remained extremely naive in her personal life. "She just believed no one would ever hurt her," he said.

Their informant continued to tell Burke and Palombo about the alleged murder. Leaving the airport in his car that night, Lenny told Joan he was the owner of several boats and that he needed some important papers from one of them. Would she mind him stopping at the waterfront, on the way to Cambridge? According to the informant, Lenny brought her aboard, killed Joan, raped her—then sunk his boat "somewhere in the harbor."

When originally questioned, Paradiso claimed his boat, The Malafemmena, had been stolen from the Pier 7 dock in South Boston and, presumably, sunk. He had filed insurance claims on the boat and all its equipment.

On the basis of the new intelligence, the State Police obtained a search warrant for the house owned by the parents of Lenny Paradiso's girlfriend, where the Quahog lived off and on.

With Detective Andy Palombo, and Troopers Bill Johnson and Richard Barrett, I conducted the search at the Revere address. We hoped to find some physical evidence to corroborate the informant's tale and tie Paradiso to the crime. Or at least something to help us locate the boat.

A search of the attic revealed a cache of expensive marine equipment. We found a depth finder, a compass and a marine radio—all reported on the insurance claim as having been missing with the stolen Malafemmena.

As we searched Lenny's room, I remember scanning the titles of a small collection of books and spotting one that seemed entirely out of place, a volume on Mayan culture and architecture. The book stuck out like a sore thumb. The other books were all on practical topics like marine engine repair, seamanship and hunting.

I'd visited a display of Mayan artifacts at the Museum of Science and remembered some of them were on loan from Harvard. Harvard had had an archaeological dig in Mexico going back to the 1920s. Given the Harvard connection and the Webster girl's interest in architecture, I sat down on Lenny Paradiso's bed and made out an affidavit for another warrant. The local clerk of courts, Joseph Faretra, came to the house and granted us the second warrant, allowing us to take from the house the book and photos of the Malafemmena.

The book, *Monuments of Civilization: The Maya*, described the architecture of the Mexican Indians. Detective Palombo confirmed Joan Webster had been scheduled to take a course in ancient cultures and architecture, including Mayan, at the graduate school of design. Paradiso, meanwhile, in whose collection the book resided, had made it through the eighth grade before dropping out.

The investigators in Burke's office established that the book was available in very few places. The only place in the Cambridge area that had it was the MIT Coop. Interviews with Joan Webster's friends, backed up with register receipts from her apartment, showed she'd shopped at the Coop, and that her purchases included books.

Lenny the Quahog was questioned again about his whereabouts on the date of Webster's disappearance, and how he happened to own a book on Mayan culture. He refused to answer on the grounds of self-incrimination.

We sought help in this case from many quarters. Reward posters with pictures of the missing boat were distributed to all the fishing and lobstering hangouts around the Boston area, as well as all pleasure boat marinas. Some commercial fisherman or weekend sailor may have sighted the boat, or snagged his nets on underwater debris that could be a sunken boat and simply failed to report it.

As a member of the State Police underwater diving team, I knew we would be called into action once we'd uncovered the marine gear. The focus of a good part of the state's investigation swung to Paradiso's boat, the Malafemmena. The informant had placed Joan Webster alive last on Lenny's boat. It was then reasoned that if the boat could be found, the body of Joan Webster may be found with it.

Our diving team was stationed at Logan primarily because the airport's approaches are over water, and we were instantly on hand in the event of a crash. We also assisted local departments throughout the Commonwealth by locating bodies and stolen cars. It's a habit with bad guys to dump cars with corpses in them into deep quarries as well as lakes and ponds. We also fulfilled various diving assignments in and around Boston Harbor for the Navy and Coast Guard.

One of the many who volunteered their help in the Webster case was Harold "Doc" Edgerton, world-famous MIT professor and developer of the strobe light. Doc Edgerton had also invented a side-scan underwater sonar. He'd located many sunken wrecks with his innovative sonar, including the Civil War ironclad ship familiar to generations of American schoolchildren, the Monitor. Sunk during a winter storm off the coast of South Carolina over a hundred years earlier, the ironclad had long been considered irretrievable. Doc Edgerton now employed the same equipment he'd used to locate wrecks in Israel and Africa in the waters near Winthrop and the saltwater Saugus river which drained past the area where the body of Marie Ianuzzi and the wallet and purse of Joan Webster had been found.

We tried several different underwater methods. Doc Edgerton's sonar was trailed behind a boat moving at five knots, while he interpreted the resultant diagram of the bottom. Hopes rose every time Doc ordered the boat stopped and sent the divers down for a closer look at the bottom.

Leo Gerstel and I even had ourselves towed along the ocean bottom off Nahant. An owner of a lobster boat had reported spotting a sunken cabin cruiser while he was pulling his lobster pots. We had him tow us on a bar, back and forth over the area—but still nothing. During the following months we dove and checked out every reported sighting. Several wrecks were found but none we wanted. The Atlantic wasn't yielding the Malafemmena.

Meanwhile, crank letters and wild leads poured into the investigation office. Each one had to be thoroughly checked out. Andy Palombo had taken the Mayan book to upstate New York, hoping for a positive ID from Joan's schoolyear roommate, but she saw nothing about the book to identify it as specifically Joan's.

Andy repeatedly went back to his informant to go over and over the story, hoping to hear something different or something he hadn't previously noted. Every time the informant got to the part about the boat, he stressed Paradiso's bragging and how emphatic Lenny the Quahog was that the boat would never be found.

As positive and dogged an investigator as Andy Palombo was, even he was beginning to think maybe the Quahog was right.

17. Evil Woman

Knowing it and proving it are two different things ...

Time: 1983
Location: Boston Harbor
Duty: Not a tea party

By the fall of 1983 it seemed discouragingly true that despite the mountain of circumstantial evidence in the Joan Webster case, the state could never obtain a conviction of Lenny the Quahog without the *corpus delicti*. All the testimony and much of the evidence led the investigators to believe that if they could find the boat, they'd find the body. Without the boat and the evidence they hoped to obtain from it, the state had no case against Lenny the Quahog.

Andy Palombo and I were pals, occasional work partners and co-owners of a sailboat. We did a lot of our brainstorming aboard the sailboat. Andy balanced my impetuousness. He could always wait me out. All during 1983 Andy Palombo was constantly bugging me to use the trooper diving team for yet another harbor search. We were crossing the harbor looking for gas for the auxiliary one Sunday when he made his final pitch. I balked.

"Andy, we've dived everywhere but off the Georges Banks, for cripes sakes. I've pulled so much trash out of Boston Harbor, the environmentalists are making me Man of the Year."

Andy smiled patiently, as always. "The guy that runs the dry dock at Pier 7—the pier where Lenny the Quahog used to berth his *Malafemmena*? Says he hit something when he was lowering the dry dock floor."

"So?"

"So, that could be where Lenny pulled the plug on his boat! The night of Joan Webster's disappearance was rough out on the water. Maybe he couldn't handle taking the boat out alone and just sunk her right at the dock."

I tried to avoid Andy's stare while I reviewed all I knew about the case. Palombo and D.A. Burke were convinced they had their murderer in Leonard Paradiso. In addition to all the previous evidence, and data from reliable informants, they'd found some extremely damning circumstantial stuff that couldn't be made public yet. Plus, the FBI had seized a purse from a bank safety deposit box registered to Paradiso and his girlfriend. Joan Webster's former roommate swore it was identical to a purse Webster had owned. Nor was the identification a fluke; the roommate had chosen the purse from what was literally a line-up of several similar purses.

"If you won't dive," Andy threatened, "I'll use Boston PD, or Metro divers."

I figured he was bluffing, but I knew also that they'd recently had their biggest breakthrough in the case when the D.A. got a letter from a prison inmate claiming the Quahog had bragged to him about killing both Ianuzzi and Joan Webster.

The prison informant who was relaying Lenny's confession to the authorities wasn't exactly from Mr. Rogers' Neighborhood himself. But he wasn't asking for special treatment and had no personal axe to grind in this case. It just seemed that the Quahog disgusted even him. The prison informant told Burke and Palombo that Paradiso bragged about the murder of Joan Webster. The Quahog told him he'd promised Webster a ride from the airport to Cambridge but took her instead to the dock at Pier 7.

Once aboard the boat, Paradiso allegedly smashed her over the head with a whiskey bottle, killing her. He then took the body far out into Boston Harbor where he dumped it overboard. It wasn't beyond Paradiso to feed the informant enough truth to make him credible to the D.A., then lie about the rest to lead the authorities astray. If it were the case that Paradiso did dump her body out beyond the harbor, or that he sunk the boat out there, the chances of finding either were virtually nil. The informant also said that during the attack on Webster, Paradiso had hurt his hand. The

D.A.'s office had records from a Lynn hospital showing Paradiso was treated for an injury to his left hand two days after the Webster disappearance. He added that Paradiso told him he sunk his boat two days after the murder.

Now Andy Palombo pushed me to dive again, hoping the Malafemmena (a translation of "evil woman") could be found under or near Pier 7, Paradiso's former docking space.

"Diving in that part of the harbor's like sticking your head in a pot of pea soup with sunglasses on," I said.

The polluted inner harbor is over thirty-five feet deep at that point, and the currents are continually shifting, so the water is murky enough to be lightless even on a bright day.

"Besides, the pier owner had a diver down there already. Nothing. And Eric Hahn's pulled several sunken cars from there: again, nothing," I said, naming the Boston Police Harbormaster who had been ultra-cooperative with us staties.

"Well, they're willing to go again," Palombo said.

"Call them then; let them do the dive."

"Tim Burke already did," Big Andy said, grinning. "They're going in at ten in the morning." He had me. And he knew it.

If our state police diving unit didn't make this dive and the Malafemmena were found, there'd be hell to pay from the higher-ups who'd allowed us time for all the other, nonproductive, dives. And it just wouldn't be fair to the crew. They'd all contributed too much time and energy not to at least be there when the boat was found.

"Okay," I said, surrendering. "But I'm not looking forward to the jurisdictional arguments if the boat *is* found—with three departments all looking for the lion's share of the glory."

We were aboard the seventy-foot Massport fireboat *Howard P. Fitzpatrick* by 0700 hours the next morning. When Troopers Sullivan, Chamberlain and Long had stowed their diving gear, we headed out of our slip in East Boston, across the harbor toward Pier 7. Intentionally three hours early, we steamed past the empty pier, out toward the mouth of the harbor. We had another assignment before diving for the Malafemmena.

The master of the Soviet ship *NovoGrodnok* (New City of Peace) had requested divers to check the hull of his ship berthed out at Castle Island. The Coast Guard had dropped the request in my lap.

"Explosives," the Coast Guard said. "Their captain's afraid the hull of his ship has been mined."

"Charming," I replied sarcastically.

"The longshoremen on the Boston docks refuse to unload her. Anti-Russian feelings are running high because of KAL flight 007, the Korean Airlines plane carrying U.S. citizens shot down over the sea of Japan after straying into Soviet airspace. He's got good reason to be nervous."

The captain of the *Fitzpatrick*, George Nashawaty, expertly slid us alongside the Russian ship and tied up. To relieve the Russian captain's fears and, possibly, to keep him from blowing up, our task was to carry out an inspection of his vessel below the water-line. Tom Chamberlain, Steve Long and Henry Sullivan got into their gear and checked each other's equipment before diving. The underwater strategy was for Trooper Henry Sullivan to swim under the keel, stern to bow, looking for anything attached to the hull of the ship that didn't belong there. Steve Long would do the same thing the length of the starboard side, while Tom Chamberlain was responsible for the portside. Diving is dangerous work, even when you're not looking for explosives, but it sure beats driving back and forth along the same stretch of highway.

After inspecting the ship, the divers would examine the pilings at dockside. While the divers were under, Sergeant Mike Foley conducted a surface inspection of the dock area. We all did a visual check while staying alert for any needs of the divers. I couldn't dive because my yearly bout with ragweed had chosen that day for its onset. I could barely breathe above water.

Our three divers reappeared near the bow of the Russian ship, about five hundred feet from the *Fitzpatrick*. They signaled all was kosher underwater, and we hauled them onto the diving platform. Mike Foley informed the Russian captain he wouldn't be going to Soviet heaven that day. A relieved Captain Nashawaty took us back into the harbor and Pier 7.

At 0930 our divers met on the pier with divers from the Boston PD and the Metropolitan District Commission. The Mets need a marine division because they have responsibility for several inland lakes and reservoirs, as well as the Boston Harbor islands. The Boston PD divers, under highly respected Harbormaster Sergeant Eric Hahn, patrol the inner harbor, responsible for all piers not under federal or Massachusetts Port Authority jurisdiction. You wonder why I smelled a jurisdictional dispute in the offing?

The three groups of divers waited in separate clumps while we worked out the details. It was finally decided that Hahn and a Boston diver would handle the area near the dry dock, and the Mets and state divers would work the area near the pier.

Sergeant Hahn was already working underwater while the other divers were still preparing their equipment. I watched a couple of the Met divers go in, then turned to see Hahn on the surface, waving me to him. I ran across the wooden piers and jumped onto the deck of the dry dock above Hahn and about thirty feet from where he was floating atop the scummy water. He'd inflated his buoyancy compensator and removed his facemask. Smiling, he jabbed a finger at the yellow Pelican buoy bobbing near him.

"Cabin cruiser, Dave—about the right size. Could be the Malafemmena!"

The other divers swarmed around the area marked by the yellow buoy. The air was charged with tension and hope. No one was as tense as Andy Palombo, standing off to one side, waiting while Eric Hahn and a diver from each department descended to attempt further identification of the sunken boat.

Palombo's tension was easily understandable. At this point, the state had no case beyond circumstantial evidence and the testimony of informants. It had no body, and virtually no physical evidence placing the suspect at the scene of the crime—anything normally necessary to convict in cases where there are no witnesses.

After what seemed an eternity, Nick Saggese, the Boston PD diver, surfaced.

"It's blue and white," he shouted. "And we can read the name ...it's...Malafemmena!"

Our cheering had barely died down when the brass of the Boston and Metro departments began showing up in heavy numbers at pierside. I guess we were lucky, because their arrival was coincidental with the media people, giving the news-teams from the major TV stations case experts to interview.

The media drew spectators. With arrivals from the D.A.'s office and everyone else, we had a pretty good crowd, all hoping to see the Malafemmena. That was going to take a while. The boat was thirty five feet down, covered with almost two years of tidal mud and silt.

After much consultation among departments, Metro sent for their air bag unit from Central Services Division. They had experience using air bags to upright jackknifed oil trucks overturned on the central artery. But the unit arrived and explained that even if the air bags worked they couldn't guarantee the rate of ascent. If raised too fast, the old Chris-craft might catapult out of the water or break apart on the way up. Valuable evidence could be lost.

Once the massaging of bruised egos was concluded, it was decided to place canvas and rubber slings under the boat and gentle it up to where it could be slid onto the flooded dry dock. From there it could be raised to the surface and pumped out. Slower but safer—for the boat. It was dangerous as hell for the divers, either way.

First the divers had to attach the slings. That meant hand-digging in the muck underneath the boat by teams of divers in relays. It was pitch-dark down there, and light from underwater lamps couldn't pierce the slit.

Eric Hahn was responsible for the work below while I coordinated the surface operation. Diver Charlie McKinnon was one of three assigned to hand-search for evidence in the muck around the boat before we tried moving it.

"Too bad the ragweed keeps you from coming down with us, Dave," he said facetiously.

"Can't think of any place I'd rather be, Charlie," I answered, just as facetiously. "Al Balestra and Joe Crowley can take turns holding your hand down there, if you're nervous. I'll be thinking of you while I'm having coffee."

Despite the banter, I was extremely relieved when those three surfaced safely. In a solid hour of perilous, blind hand-searching through the muck around the Malafemmena, they'd found nothing to help Palombo's case.

By late afternoon the boat was moved onto the dry dock, raised and the pumping out begun. On that night's six o'clock news millions of Boston-area viewers caught flood-lit glimpses of the emerging Malafemmena and speculated what secrets were aboard.

By the next morning water still poured from the sea cocks and portholes. Barnacles and slimy sea-growth crusted the outside, and thick, oozing mud choked the interior. To the chagrin of the authorities connected with the case, it was immediately ascertained that Joan Webster's body was not aboard.

Still hoping for other physical evidence, we carefully hoisted the Malafemmena onto a flatbed, covered it with canvas and towed it under police escort to Pier 1 on the East Boston side of the harbor, near the airport. Once safely locked inside the pier and dried out, state and FBI crime lab crews and forensic experts would spend days on the boat sifting and sorting through the debris. They sent questionable material to the FBI lab in Washington for more exhaustive analysis. All legal means were pursued in hopes of bringing Paradiso to justice.

Andy Palombo even got our trooper crew to dive around Pier 7 again with a device like an underwater vacuum cleaner. Two months of underwater work sifting all the harbor silt around where they'd found the Malafemmena brought new meaning to the word patience. Still nothing was found that would corroborate the evidence against Lenny the Quahog.

The best shot the state had was to try to tie what physical evidence they had, along with the testimony of informants, to a sliver of glass they hoped to find in the thumb of Lenny the Quahog.

The jail tipster had sworn that Paradiso told him the treatment at Lynn hospital had been for a cut on his thumb, suffered when the whiskey bottle that he allegedly killed his victim with broke. Supposedly, a sliver of that glass remained in Paradiso's thumb. The state hoped to match the glass in his thumb with broken glass discovered on the Malafemmena. All other evidence was circumstantial; would this sliver of glass be sufficient to prosecute Paradiso?

"We got that thrown out," said Brookline attorney Rick Dyer, then a member of Paradiso's defense team. "The D.A. couldn't prove if whatever had been in Paradiso's thumb had actually come from a whiskey bottle, or what. I don't blame him for trying, but I think Burke wanted Paradiso so badly, he was taking longshots with evidence he might not normally have tried to prosecute with."

Tim Burke's boss, Suffolk County District Attorney Newman Flanagan, later said, "We feel we know what happened [to Joan Webster], but knowing it and proving it are two different things."

When Tim Burke recently resigned from the D.A.'s office to start his own practice, it was felt that would end the prosecution of Paradiso on the Webster case. But D.A. Flanagan avers that if new evidence is ever found, Burke will be brought back as a special prosecutor.

"I'm not leaving this case," Burke confirms. "I'll never stop working on this one."

Trooper Andy Palombo feels the same way.

18. Dope Dive

Why were you running without lights?

Time: Recent
Location: Logan International
Duty: Drug traffic

Sergeant Al Rivet spied the flashing light of the alarm phone. Reaching across the duty desk at Troop F headquarters, he grabbed his dispatch mike to alert the trooper nearest the alarm location.

"Control to zone 3. Covert alarm—Delta security checkpoint."

Trooper Frank Hommel acknowledged over his hand-held portable as he walked quickly through the North Terminal toward the Delta gate. Even down the long airport passageway he could spot the metal detector and conveyer belt so familiar in airports worldwide.

Frank Hommel walked even faster, wondering if it was another concealed weapon alarm. The political terrorist activity endemic to modern life had made bomb and weapon searches a normal phase of passenger processing. Airports around the world were beefing up antiterrorist security even before the Libyan situation. But as security searches increased and stiffened, dedicated criminals, political and otherwise, became more sophisticated at hiding weapons and explosives. Logan, a major point of international departure and entry, is a natural conduit for clandestine activity.

There is no perfect system, but troopers, working with U.S. Customs, the Drug Enforcement Administration and the FBI, manage to catch their share of illegal traffickers. Several detection methods are employed, including metal sensors, dogs and luggage

X-ray. The common walk-through detector is the one seen by most travelers. At Logan, if the X-rays pick out the shape of a weapon or suspicious material in the luggage, the airline security agent rings a silent alarm for Troop F. Like this call.

Trooper Hommel took in the situation. Off to the side of the checkpoint a young Delta security agent was engaged in debate with a Hispanic male, about twenty-five. He held a briefcase typical of carry-on luggage for business travelers. Relieved to see Hommel arrive, the agent gave a nervous smile.

"Trooper. This gentleman refuses permission to inspect his hand luggage."

Hommel relaxed his guard somewhat. This wasn't a weapons call or, by procedure, the agent would have immediately mentioned any suspicion of a firearm or explosive. In Spanish, he asked the suspect his name.

"*Me llamo Jose Colon*—and I can speak English," the suspect answered. Hommel couldn't tell if he were more angry or nervous.

"English then." Hommel gestured at the briefcase. "This your bag, Jose?"

Jose nodded.

"There's a sign as you enter the security area stating that when you decide to pass through here, you are giving us permission to open all luggage. Did you read that sign, Mr. Colon?"

Jose nodded again, his eyes darting from side to side.

"What's inside?" Hommel asked.

"Paper, just some papers is all."

"Will you open it now, please?"

At Hommel's insistence, Jose reluctantly unlatched the attaché case. His reluctance was understandable; filling all space inside were thick, green, neatly stacked bundles of U.S. currency. Money for a drug buy.

Trooper John Kelley responded to Hommel's request for a detective. Immediately after taking over the questioning of Jose Colon, Kelley could see why this suspect had been stopped. Jose fit a profile. Here was an Hispanic male, nervous as a bridegroom, trying to get past security with a brand-new briefcase full of money.

Jose had all the wrong answers for detective Kelley's opening questions. Kelley brought the suspect to the station for further questioning and a count of the money in front of witnesses. If not returned to him after questioning, Jose would be given a receipt for the money. Carmen Tammaro was the NCOIC of the Troop F detective unit.

"Got us another mule, Sarge," Kelley announced, escorting Jose in.

It took twenty minutes for Tammaro to tally the stacks while Kelley witnessed the count. Fifty thousand dollars.

To repeated questions the mule, Jose Colon, continued to insist the money wasn't for a drug deal. Unemployed, holding a one-way ticket to Miami, Jose was simply taking the money south for a friend. Sure. People do it every day. Instead of mailing checks, or using banks to transfer funds, they throw fifty thou into a brief-case and have someone like Jose swing it down on a plane for them. Sure.

Though it didn't appear to be so in Jose's case, not every mule is a criminal. Some of them are people unaware of what they are carrying. They honestly think they are simply doing a favor for a friend. They naively jump at a chance for a free ticket south without asking too many careful questions.

But most mules are like Jose; they know what they're doing. Mules either carry the money to finance drug buys or transport the drugs purchased. They are generally paid between two and five hundred dollars per trip, plus their ticket. Airport detectives like Andy Palombo have sometimes caught the same mule several times. Tammaro returned the greenbacks to the briefcase.

"Didn't you tell the trooper this was just paper?"

"I forgot the money was in there. A friend gave me it to take to Florida for him."

"What's the friend's name, Jose?" Kelley asked.

"I forget."

Jose also couldn't remember the address of the friend who had entrusted him with fifty thousand dollars, nor his phone number. He *did* remember the friend didn't trust banks.

The troopers seized the fifty thousand dollars as contraband. Jose agreed to the count, accepted a receipt signed by both officers and went on his way. After so many similar grabs, Carmen and John were used to the nonchalant manner of someone walking away from a small fortune. Profits from illicit drugs are so astronomically high that risks like this are taken several times a day.

Kelley stuffed the money into the safe while Tammaro called Newman Flanagan's people in the Suffolk County D.A.'s office, informing them of the seizure. Based on past experience, some high-priced criminal attorney would call making inquiries about the impounded funds less than an hour from the time Jose hit the street.

Seldom was he successful in retrieving the money. The troopers would refer the attorney to the D.A.'s office, who would in turn request a superior court hearing to ascertain the true owner of the funds. That usually did it. The real client wants to remain anonymous, and the mules can't usually offer much more of a reason for carrying all that cash except that it was a deposit on some real estate. Lots of real estate being purchased in Miami by unemployed mules...

When the mule doesn't get caught, the money gets to Miami, he gets the rest of his fee, and he's finished with that transaction. Someone else is hired to drive a nondescript five-year-old Florida car up to Massachusetts or New York. Sometimes the cars are sold at wholesale auctions when they arrive to throw the heat off the track, then picked up again later. Other times they are taken directly to body shops for dismemberment and disposal. In any case those cars pay for themselves hundreds of times over with the payload of cocaine they transported north, expertly concealed somewhere in the body.

Another favorite ploy is to insert the drugs within the manifest of a regulation air freight shipment. After unloading, the shipment of ostensibly innocent freight, anything from furniture to shell jewelry, is routinely called for at the freight office, then driven out of the airport.

Hoping to at least slow down the flow of illicit drugs into Boston, the State Police works closely with the DEA and U.S. Customs officers at the airport. They also maintain daily contact with other drug agents in New York, Montreal and Miami, and trade information with police from around the world.

John Kelley looked up from writing his report to see Carmen Tammaro pacing the floor of the detective's office.

"John, we only grab a *fraction* of the money that leaves Boston for drug buys. We know that. Yet in the last couple of months alone we've caught dozens of mules like this Jose, and we've seized at least three times more money headed out than we normally intercept."

Kelley nodded his agreement. Tammaro pointed at Kelley with his cigar.

"But at the same time, we're seizing only the normal amount of drugs *coming in*. And we haven't radically altered our methods of detection, one way or the other."

"Meaning?" Kelley asked.

"Meaning, the money goes out of here to purchase the drugs that are brought back in here. There's a ratio."

"Gotcha"

"But lately the ratio is way out of balance. The big numbers we're seizing says there's lots of cash going out, but only the same old amount of drugs coming back in. Can only mean one thing."

"They're piling up money somewhere. For a big score."

"Right—there's a monster drug shipment coming our way."

"When?"

"Kel', if I knew that, I'd be retired on my lottery winnings. I wouldn't be here trying to teach you the finer points of crimebusting."

While Tammaro and Kelley were finishing up their report on the mule, another phase of the troopers' Logan drug watch was unfolding near the New York shuttle ramp.

Trooper Bill Johnson and DEA agent Herb Lemmon were waiting, watching arrival preparations for the eight o'clock shuttle very closely. The one-hour Boston to New York shuttle was one of the first services of its type where the traveler could just hop aboard without reservations and pay his fare en route.

NYPD had alerted Boston. One of their drug dogs had hit on a bag at Eastern's baggage hold area in New York, but, unable to determine the owner, they let it go out on the shuttle. A yellow tag had been tied on the bag so it could be readily identified at arrival in Boston, where its claimant would be taken into custody.

The ringing bells of the jetway as it swiveled into position signaled the shuttle's arrival. Trooper Johnson and Agent Lemmon mingled with the crowd as it spilled from the jetway corridor. Pacing themselves to appear as if they'd been on the shuttle, they joined the flow of commuters rushing toward the baggage area. Caught up in the headlong plunge toward the baggage carousel, Trooper Bill Johnson had to smile to himself. From his own travel experience and his work at the airport, he knew there was nothing gained by rushing to the baggage carousels; it rarely took the ramp crew less than twenty minutes to unload the A300 airbus and get the baggage to the conveyor. Nonetheless, people jostled their fellow travelers, speeding from the plane to the carousel, only to stand there waiting at the empty conveyor.

Agent Herb Lemmon took a position near the door while Bill Johnson moved among the crowd. As the conveyor started around, they tried to melt into the background. Neither officer could help trying to guess which member of the crowd would turn out to be the smuggler. Would it be a housewife out for a day of shopping, or a salesman? Waiting were executives, students, even Hassidic gold and gem merchants. Who amongst them would be the drug carrier?

As the jumbled baggage began to circle, they strained for a glimpse of the yellow tag. Trooper Johnson spotted it first; he signaled Lemmon at the door. They watched as the large brown suitcase circled. And circled. No one made a move for it. Johnson thought the yellow BOS tag was a dead giveaway. Had it alarmed the smuggler already? Had he spotted it amongst all the white tags and abandoned the dope?

The luggage circled again, the tag becoming even more noticeable as other travelers pulled their bags off and departed the carousel area.

The man who finally reached for the luggage blew all of Johnson's preconceptions. Tall and trim in an expensive gray business suit and horn-rimmed glasses, he looked to Johnson like a stockbroker. They were just about to nab the guy when he suddenly lifted his hand from the yellow-tagged luggage and stepped back from the carousel. Johnson and Lemmon waited, frustrated.

The stockbroker walked away from the luggage conveyor. Was it a mistake? He circled back and watched the bag make two more revolutions, then strode quickly to the carousel, snatching the bag as he moved for the exit. No mistake.

When Johnson and Lemmon closed in on him outside the claim area he dropped the bag, denying he owned it.

"In that case," said Herb. "We got you for larceny from a building, for stealing the bag."

As Agent Lemmon turned the suspect to the wall for frisking, Trooper Johnson spied a crumpled piece of paper fall from the suspect's fingers. Johnson tromped on it before the wind carried it off. The baggage claim check!

The claim check gave them solid evidence to use in court to prove the suspect luggage did indeed belong to the stockbroker and that holding him was justified. They couldn't open the luggage without a search warrant, and a search warrant couldn't be obtained without probable cause. The way recent court rulings were going, they weren't sure if the New York tip-off would stand as probable cause. If the guy simply denied everything, they were probably sunk.

Johnson and Lemmon brought their cuffed suspect and his brown bag to Troop F for further questioning. They had just seated him in the office, when Corporal Greg Studley happened to walk through with "Baron," his drug-trained German Shepherd sniff dog. Nearing the stockbroker and his brown bag, Baron almost tore the leash from Corporal Studley's hands trying to get at the bag. Now a search warrant was no problem.

The suspect was a broker all right, but his product wasn't traded over the counter. In his bag the authorities discovered two kilos of 70 percent pure cocaine. Estimated eventual street value of two kilos after it's been cut and measured—approximately half a million dollars.

It had been a good night for the good guys.

While Sergeant Tammaro was pointing his cigar at detective John Kelley and trying to think himself a step ahead of the local drug operation, the 120-foot Coast Guard cutter *Bar Harbor* was plowing through the ocean swells seventy nautical miles east of Portland, Maine.

The duty officer on the *Bar Harbor*, Lieutenant Paul Perochi, was delighted to be heading back to port in Boston after his annual two-week active duty Naval Reserve cruise. A high school teacher in "real life," Perochi was relaxing with a book when the boatswain called him to the ship's bridge.

"Looks like a coastal freighter, sir; running without lights. Heading about 270," the boatswain reported, pointing into the predawn darkness.

Perochi squinted, trying to catch a silhouette of the freighter on the hazy horizon. All commercial vessels were required to show lights. Those that didn't were either in trouble mechanically or avoiding being seen. Unable to spot the vessel with his naked eye, Perochi switched to the radar screen.

"Change course to 250," he ordered, sighting the rogue vessel. "Increase speed to 20 knots."

"Should I try to raise him by radio, sir? He's required to monitor channel 16."

"Let's close in on him first in case he decides to run," Perochi said. "If his lights were legitimately malfunctioning, anyone with half a brain would show emergency lights of some type, for safety's sake."

Approaching from the east, by 0445 hours the cutter had closed to within four hundred yards. The dawn's early light backlighted them on the gray horizon. The darkened freighter's red and green running lights suddenly blinked on as the cutter neared.

"He saw us, Wilson—raise him, request his name and registry."

"Coast Guard cutter *Bar Harbor* whiskey yankee zebra 117, to vessel ahead...please identify yourself," the boatswain radioed.

They repeated the call twice. No answer. Suspicions rising, Perochi sent for the skipper of his ship, a regular Navy Lieutenant. Several minutes elapsed before a British voice crackled over the radio: "Motor vessel *Ramsland*, Liberian registry."

Perochi had them switch from the emergency band to channel 22.

"Prepare for a boarding party."

He had just rung general quarters when the commander of the *Bar Harbor* appeared on the bridge. He heard Perochi's hurried account, then gave the go-ahead to board.

While the Coast Guard boarding party inspected the crew quarters and cargo hold of the *Ramsland*, Perochi checked the ship's papers. The master of the Liberian freighter told Paul Perochi he was heading the ship to Boston where it would be cut up for scrap.

"Why were you running without lights?"

"Generator problems. The engineer had to douse the lights temporarily for repairs."

The chief petty officer in charge of the search reported he found nothing out of line in the quarters and that the hold was empty except for the crushed stone used as ballast. Perochi still felt the captain was lying, but he had no legitimate reason to question the master further. He and his crew were politely escorted to the side. They reluctantly returned to the *Bar Harbor* where he reported to the captain.

"Something fishy there. Outside, that scow looks like it's ready for the scrapheap. But down below doesn't jive with the exterior. It looks too new. Everything's just too neat for the average merchant ship."

The captain of the *Bar Harbor* promised the reservist he'd discuss Perochi's suspicions with the customs people in Boston. That's where I came in. The Coast Guard got to customs and customs asked the State Police for diving help. My commander, Captain Gilbert Frechette, sent the diving crew to rendezvous with customs and the CG.

For all I knew at that point, we could've been checking for bombs, as we had on the Russian ship, or illegal aliens or South American lichen. All Captain Frechette had told me was that customs was keeping an eye on a ship anchored in Boston Harbor, and they'd requested an inspection of the hull.

The *Ramsland* was tied up behind the 310-foot cutter *Sherman*. Pulling in, I saw an experienced detective, Sergeant Mike Foley, already huddled with the CG and customs officials. Eventually the chief customs inspector detached himself from the group and filled me in while my crew unloaded our van.

"We think this *Ramsland* is a drug boat, but we haven't been able to find a damn thing. We want you to inspect her thoroughly below the waterline before we give up the ghost."

"If it's clean, what makes you think it's a drug transport?" I asked.

"They'd be *losing* money, coming here with an empty hold just to scrap her. Economically, it doesn't add up." The inspector told me how the ship had aroused Paul Perochi's suspicions running without lights. "We've gone over everything. The hold is empty except for ballast, and there's nowhere else they could hide any quantity. Check the keel for any marks of recent soldering. Maybe they opened an airtight compartment between the hull and the interior plates."

"Gotcha."

"Our patrol boat's at your disposal."

Our diving crew loaded their gear onto the CG forty-one-footer. Troopers Charlie McKinnon and Steve Long were assigned the starboard side of the suspect vessel. They'd check out the keel by swimming under and along the side of the ship nearest the pier. Divers Leo Gerstel and Steve Lynch would handle the port side, from bow to stern. I was supervising the dive from the deck of the *Ramsland*.

While we worked, CG and customs people had boarded the *Ramsland* and anxiously watched the progression of air bubbles along the side of the ship. I say anxiously because they had committed a lot of government time and money to this search. Not that every drug search is expected to successfully yield drugs, but nobody likes to have a hunch proven wrong.

As the divers surfaced, I left the Liberian ship to take their reports out of earshot of the captain and crew.

"Nothing, Dave" was the consensus from our divers.

These were experienced underwater men as well as troopers who knew what they were looking for when it came to hidden drugs. All the plate seams on the keel looked like the originals. I was confident of their judgment. Returning to the bridge of the Liberian freighter, I delivered the negative report to the officials.

Customs and Coast Guard dejectedly pondered shutting down the operation. Looking down into an open cargo hatch, Foley remarked on the ballast of gravel-sized stone that covered the floor of the hold.

"Looks like the expressway, under repair," Foley quipped, his expression thoughtful. "What say, as a last shot, we lower a drug dog down into the hold for a sniff search? Maybe a dog could smell something we couldn't see. Whattaya got to lose?" Foley shrugged.

When Corporal Greg Studley arrived with Baron, a sling was fixed around the nervous dog's middle and he was lowered down into the ship's bowels.

Baron began yelping even before his legs touched down. Immediately upon landing in the hold he started clawing wildly, trying to dig a hole through the stone ballast. Mike Foley looked as surprised as anyone else. *Something* was down there.

A Coast Guard work crew dropped into the hold. Starting where Baron had led them, they dug, using large sheets of plywood as shoring to keep the stone from sliding back in on them. Baron's frantic howls continued over the clatter of shovels on stone, spurring them on. After an hour's fierce digging they had a hole three feet deep. The diggers felt something underfoot.

Baron nearly broke his leash a few minutes later when what looked like the tops of cotton bales began to appear beneath the shovels. The cause for his frenzy was quickly obvious. The bottom of the *Ramsland* was stuffed with huge bales of marijuana.

That was only the beginning. Combined crews from the various agencies had to dig around the clock to uncover all the pot. When finished, they had hauled out a hundred bales of dope. The largest seizure of marijuana ever on the east coast had been pulled from Boston Harbor.

When news of the incredible arrest and seizure reached the Troop F detective's office, Carmen Tammaro had his answer. Now he knew where all the extra drug money was going. It was going to purchase the *Ramsland* and its cargo of weed.

Epilogue

By the end of my career I had come full circle—Troop A headquarters, Framingham, Massachusetts. On the same turf that I had sweated out my first sixteen weeks as a potential trooper, my eye on Route 9, I now walked comfortably as a lieutenant in the Massachusetts State Police. I'd come a long way.

I now practice law in Somerville, Massachusetts, but I still think of my trooper experiences nearly every day. For over twenty years I covered nearly every kind of assignment the force had to offer, from the most rural mountain towns to the most hectic city neighborhoods. But the people that I met offered even greater variety. From the lowest criminal to the kindest people I could ever meet, the range of types I encountered while on duty provided me with a lasting education in human nature.

My career was not atypical. The State Police, with its fascinating variety of assignments, its rigorous training and its distinct philosophy, has fulfilled the childhood dream of many a boy and girl, rarely disappointing them. I consider myself fortunate to have shared a good portion of my life with some of the finest people in the world.

There are many things I'd like to do over in life, but being a trooper isn't one of them.

Photo credits in order of appearance:

D.W. Moran; Paul J. Driscoll; State Police Photo Bureau; *The Boston Globe; Trooper Newspaper; The Boston Globe; The Boston Globe; Trooper Newspaper; Trooper Newspaper;* Paul J. Driscoll; Paul J. Driscoll; D.W. Moran; D.W. Moran; D.W. Moran; State Police Photo Bureau; *Trooper Newspaper; Trooper Newspaper; The Boston Herald; The Boston Globe;* Trooper Thomas Chamberlain; and D.W. Moran